# INTERNATIONAL CONSTRUCTION BUSINESS MANAGEMENT

# INTERNATIONAL CONSTRUCTION BUSINESS MANAGEMENT

## A Guide for Architects, Engineers, and Contractors

### Chester L. Lucas, P.E.

**McGraw-Hill Book Company**

New York   St. Louis   San Francisco   Auckland   Bogotá   Hamburg
Johannesburg   London   Madrid   Mexico   Montreal   New Delhi
Panama   Paris   São Paulo   Singapore   Sydney   Tokyo   Toronto

**Library of Congress Cataloging in Publication Data**

Lucas, Chester L.
   International construction business management.

   Bibliography: p.
   Includes index.
   1. Construction industry—Management  2. International
business-enterprises—Management.  I. Title.
HD9715.A2L83 1985     624'.068     85-4250
ISBN 0-07- 038916-0

1234567890    DOC/DOC    898765

ISBN 0-07-038916-0

The editors for this book were Joan Zseleczky and Barbara B. Toniolo, the
designer was M. R. P. Design, and the production supervisor was Sally Fliess. It
was set in ITC Bookman Light by University Graphics, Inc.

Printed and bound by R. R. Donnelley & Sons Company.

*To Isabel and Mark—who were there*

# CONTENTS

# PREFACE

One's first assignment as a project manager abroad provides unusual challenges. In my experience, the main concerns were not Quito's high altitude, the Spanish language, the metric system, or the Andes' rugged topography. Rather, the difficult tests were related to client communications, understanding a new culture, avoiding local politics, and supervising a diverse group of senior professionals. Less difficult, but still challenging, were the tasks of collecting invoices, supervising international contractors, and satisfying the client's staff.

The professional rewards were gratifying, however. The project was completed, trust and confidence were established, and friendships were founded. My next assignment, in Panama as project manager for a farm-to-market road program, produced a few of the old challenges and many new ones. At that point, I became addicted to international consulting. There were then no available reference books dealing with management of consultants' operations. Very little hands-on advice for survival was forthcoming from any quarter. Later on, when offered an opportunity to work in Nicaragua as construction management advisor on the country's first hydroelectric project, I looked to a World Bank officer for some sage advice. His terse comment was "Equip yourself with a new attache case and a tightly rolled umbrella, and tackle the job with confidence."

Literature about the management of domestic operations for architects, engineers, construction managers, and related professionals still remains scarce. Overseas offices and foreign projects are covered, if at all, by discouraging horror stories of the "tried-it-once-and-didn't-like-it" sort.

Without reference books, it seemed wise to keep diaries and to preserve detailed trip logs as well as copies of my reports— all filed away for future reference. Each assignment brought new experiences—Panama, Nicaragua, Italy, France, Spain, Germany, Libya, Lebanon, Greece, Saudi Arabia, the Middle East, and Africa—and wove the fabric of a long engineering career. Throughout these experiences I frequently promised myself, "This one will be a chapter in the book." And finally with the encouragement of several friends, including Jim Webber of *Engineering News-Record* and *International Construction Week* and the late Dick Lurie of *Worldwide Projects* this book took form in print.

My goal is to provide positive and enthusiastic guidance— candidly and pragmatically—to professionals entering the export market. The basic premise is that the reader will be interested in international practice and, after reading this book, will be better equipped to decide whether he or she can cope with the challenges that will inevitably confront the new entrant.

The reader will find sound practical approaches for planning and executing fact-finding studies, selecting associates, marketing, presenting proposals, and negotiating contracts. Once the contract is firmly in hand, chapters on organization, project management, logistics, personnel, and financial management will provide positive guidance. In later chapters such sophisticated challenges as extras and claims, politics, bribery, and unstable conditions are discussed.

Although the primary audience is assumed to be professionals with an interest in foreign work, the material is structured for exporters, bankers, lawyers, accountants, contractors, suppliers, graduate students, and, in fact, anyone who intends to operate in another culture. In offering the reader guidance for coping successfully with the many new and challenging aspects of foreign business, I stress attitudes of awareness and understanding that will equip and encourage competent professionals to enter the market, meet the competition, and successfully complete foreign assignments.

It is my premise that an understanding of the client's problems, careful planning, and delivery of a quality product will lead to success in the overseas arena. A conscious effort has been made to refrain from pedantic solutions. Rather, I attempt to stimulate original thinking based on proven principles of operation. A rational approach to the export market coupled with enthusiastic and strong leadership will certainly bring professional and personal satisfaction to those attracted to this exciting and rewarding field.

Those who work in international engineering and construction gain long and intensive exposure to new cultures, customs, cuisines, and environments. A good knowledge of languages, history, and people is acquired, almost without conscious effort. Successful internationalists reflect enthusiasm, professional satisfaction, and pride. So, take time to appreciate the history, culture, and the great people encountered along the way. Enjoy the satisfaction of being part of the construction team, and accept gracefully the role of teacher and unofficial ambassador.

Good luck in your foreign endeavors!

### *Acknowledgments*

Without the wisdom, help, and patience of the many capable engineers, architects, planners, construction people, and devoted staff with whom I worked during a long career, there would have been nothing worth writing about. My grateful thanks to all of them.

Several chapters deal with topics that were the subject of articles written by the author and published in *Worldwide Projects,* whose publisher, Paul R. Green, and editorial director, Virginia Fairweather, have graciously given permission for the reuse of the ideas contained therein.

C. W. Gilliam and John F. Moller, friends and former associates with lengthy foreign service, have reviewed certain chapters and provided valuable comments which have added to the book's validity.

Special thanks go to Susan Schultz and Denise Roth of Larsen Associates Inc. for their support and skill in converting the handwritten pages into processed text with efficiency and understanding.

## A Note about This Book

The role of women in the design and management professions has increased dramatically in the period covered by this book. At engineering schools such as Duke University, enrollment of women has reached 30 percent and is increasing steadily. In design and construction management organizations, women are in positions at all levels. However, in the international market, and particularly in developing countries, assignments for women as resident representatives and project managers are not as common as for men for the following reasons:

1. *Experience requirements.* The usual requirement for assignment as a resident representative or project manager on a foreign contract is ten to fifteen years of relevant experience in design, management, and client relations. A professional seeking a position of the type described in Chapters 8 and 13 will have paid these "dues." Most young professionals are not willing to take this career path.

2. *Mobility concerns.* Candidates for foreign assignment are generally selected because of ease of mobility and willingness to accept the challenge of hostile environments. Two-career families and those with children in lower school grades or members who require special medical or educational support are not attracted to assignments in developing countries.

3. *Cultural differences.* In the Middle East and other developing areas, closed cultures unfortunately prescribe limited roles for women in professional life. For this reason a firm often finds obstacles to obtaining a work permit and resident visa for a manager who happens to be female.

Professional and technical positions described in this book are assumed to be open to women or men. The words "she" or "he" are meant to be interchangeable—given the required training and experience. In Chapter 8, "Your Man on the Scene," and Chapter 13, "Project Organization and the Project Manager," however, the assignments are challenging ones in any cultural environment much different from our own. It would be naive to suggest that a woman could necessarily expect to succeed as well as a man in representing a design or construction management firm in this fragile and competitive market. For this reason, these chapters are intended to indicate that the assignment is more suitable for male professionals.

I look forward to the day when women will be represented in equal numbers in international management and operations, as they have largely been on the national scene. But for the foreseeable future I believe that a prudent adviser will counsel firms entering the foreign market to be sensitive to the cultural values of the host country.

CHESTER LUCAS

# CHAPTER 1

# THE DECISION TO EXPORT

There is a broad international market for consulting engineers, architects, planners, and construction managers. The risks are at least as great as those encountered in domestic operations. Moreover, new cultures and environments will challenge patience, understanding, and ingenuity. Why should an established organization venture into the international market? What good can come from this corporate risk?

On a routine trip home from Italy in 1966, I made a presentation of a planning, design, and construction management project for a new town in Libya to a Virginia state meeting of civil engineers. The project was an ambitious one, and my pride and sense of accomplishment were obvious. Few in the audience were internationally experienced, and so there was a lively question period. I was totally unprepared, then, for the rather emotional question: "With all of the engineering needs of our country, why would any competent American engineer want to leave home and put up with all of those unfamiliar problems?"

I was taken aback. The necessity for confronting my peers on the subject had never occurred to me. Certainly when struggling with some of the least attractive conditions peculiar to foreign work—and momentarily frustrated by them—I had asked myself the same question. Yet the period of uncertainty had usually passed without aftermath, and I would seek new problems. I offered a poorly organized reply, touching on the thrill of winning an international design competition against a field of prestigious firms, the satisfaction of providing housing for earthquake victims, and the challenge of the environment and the cultural problems that arise when working, for example, with Arab clients and Polish contractors. I added that there had also been an opportunity for a profitable contract as well as for professional development. Finally—and with some mischievous intent—I pointed out that this international effort was not an alternate source of business but an addition to our domestic practice; if the questioner knew of domestic opportunities, our firm would be pleased to share his workload.

Indeed, why seek foreign contracts? The answer becomes obvious during periods of high interest rates, energy shortages, and stagnant domestic markets. Although the economies of other countries are affected by the state of the industrialized economies, the demand for design and construction services in certain international markets can be high when it is low at home. For example, oil-exporting countries are still spending huge amounts on industrial, social, and infrastructure projects. Certain other countries whose economies are based on agriculture (such as Cameroon) or minerals (such as Indonesia, Malaysia, or Colombia) have been large buyers of construction services. The fact remains that export markets can provide good opportunities when domestic markets do not offer new sources of income. Earning hard currency which can be converted into dollars, sterling, francs, or other hard currencies and brought home with taxes paid on profit is very respectable. In addition, this trade contributes to righting the balance of payments and helps put the domestic economy in the black. There is also another, perhaps less obvious benefit from exports of professional services: the export sales of construction equipment materials and installed machinery. Such sales have a direct effect on the domestic labor market which may be sorely needed. President Reagan stated in a nationally televised press conference (January 5, 1983) that for every billion dollars of export sales, forty thousand American jobs would be supported. Such benefits are a substantial part of the U.S. economy and are very significant to the Korean, Dutch, British, and French economies.

The international market, particularly in infrastructure projects for developing countries, requires large doses of very simple and basic design. Because public works in such countries are not generally maintained properly, the designer must address this problem. Otherwise, as the histories of many developing countries will bear out, dams and bridges have washed away and long stretches of a recently built highway have vanished from existence. The cause of these failures relates more to poor maintenance than to faulty design or construction. This very fact heightens the engineer's challenge and makes foreign contracts even more professionally rewarding. It is often said that the type of design most successful is simple and straightforward—similar to that which might have been in vogue at home thirty or forty years ago and with a lack of features that are hard to maintain in hostile environments.

Developing countries also present a fast-growing market for services in training, operation, and management of infrastructure projects. International airports, ports, and water and waste water treatment plants are being operated and maintained by internationl contractors in the oil-producing Middle East. Frequently, engineering firms join with industry to manage and staff these projects. Opportunities exist because of the lack of skilled and professional workers, as well as cultural differences which make service trades unacceptable to certain ethnic groups.

My goal is to provide practical procedures for establishing, organizing, and operating foreign design and construction management offices. The market offers opportunties on all sides, but international competition is fierce. The path to success is lined with pitfalls and monuments to fallen contenders. How can you determine if your firm is suited professionally and financially to enter this arena? How can ineptness be identified? Care must be taken to avoid making a poor exporter out of a great domestic organization.

The first phase is one of inventory, soul-searching, and self-analysis. If these hurdles are negotiated with enthusiasm, the next step will include market study and homework. Following the homework phase comes preparation of an operations plan and a budget for a fact-finding trip. The third phase consists of the fact-finding trip, summarizing its conclusions, making recommendations, and arriving at a budget and an operations plan for the first year of foreign activities. If the report is negative, the foreign market idea can be aborted or postponed with no great loss. If the report is positive, it can be presented to management for approval and the operation launched for a trial period. Using this rational approach avoids wasting large amounts of money and keeps management from making its commitment based on anything except hard logic. Our goal during this period is to take the "gee whiz" out of international operation by simulating an engineering problem with several unknowns and variables.

The inventory must be conducted by an individual who understands the organization from top to bottom and who has some knowledge of international operations. It would be helpful if the person chosen were a partner, shareholder, or officer. Since this phase is staff work, it would be well to keep the senior partner or president out of the picture, except in a general way, until decision-making time. (If the CEO were a great internationalist, there would be no need for this study.)

One purpose of the inventory is to identify your organization's strengths and basic resources and to determine how they relate to the needs of the international market. It is important to stress existing capabilities that can be well documented when presented to potential clients. Technocrats in rapidly developing countries want to study your track record over the past five years. Pertinent overseas experience should be researched and carefully described. Your project managers and department heads are prone to be impressed by their past efforts, so they often tend to make extravagant portrayals of the firm's experience which will not hold up under close scrutiny. For example, if a contract scope covered a feasibility study, one should not claim final design responsibility. Such pretenses are unethical, to say the least, and presentations based on dubious experience will collapse like a house of cards.

It is not necessary during "inventorying" to spend money on final preparation of resumes. Devote the time to gathering facts for an appraisal of the firm's international potential. Periods of foreign residence, ability with languages, professional registration, and education obtained abroad are typical of the facts that will be useful in the evaluation.

A frank investigation of the organization's strengths and weaknesses will complement the review of personnel and product. Now is not the time to belabor past mistakes. Honest appraisal of capability must be stated. If the firm has never designed a twenty-four-story reinforced concrete building, it may be a waste of time to try to convince a prospective client that the project should be entrusted to you. Indeed, there may be a need to strengthen the organization by the addition of specialists or associates in certain fields. It can readily be imagined that planners, economists, agronomists, educational consultants, and other talented professionals might be welcome additions to a basic engineering staff when operating in rapidly developing countries.

Another element for the inventory is to get the senior management's thoughts about prospective international markets. This survey of "first impressions" may be quite useful when the homework starts. One partner may have strong professional and family ties to a potential market area. There may be some exceptional language skills and cultural backgrounds that would be of value in Latin America, China, Africa, or the Middle East. A department head may have managed an engineering office in Europe or have been an instructor in a Kuwait university. The thoughts and preferences of the movers and shapers of your firm should be incorporated in the conclusions of the inventory. Inclusion may well heighten the interest of these individuals and their commitment to the international program. Commitment of the principals is an ingredient vital to the success of an international program, but like many other things, it is difficult to obtain and easy to lose. Take care to get the input of all the top management and directors, even if the task becomes tedious. Once involved, no individual can say he or she was not consulted. From these suggestions about inventory and self-analysis, a custom-designed list of questions can be developed for your organization. As questions are answered, new areas to be probed will be uncovered. At this stage, the intent is only to get clues to interest your firm in the potential of exporting services. The inventory should be conducted on a confidential basis by a dedicated professional. Care should be taken not to expose the idea as a target to be shot down early on. Frivolous objections should be screened out of the analysis. The fact that the senior partner picked up dysentery in Cairo should not be sufficient grounds to keep the firm out of the Middle East.

With the results in hand, conclusions can be made. The inventory should be carefully tabulated, checked for accuracy in critical areas, and digested into a short report to management. Assuming that the results show the firm to be a potential contender in the export market, you should make a proposal to

enter the homework phase. No airplane tickets should be pur-
chased yet, or European tours contemplated. During the homework period the fact-finding trip will be planned and budgeted.
Now the search and struggle for corporate commitment will
begin.

# CHAPTER 2

# HOMEWORK— THE MARKET STUDY

The results of the inventory will probably not be surprising, although new perspectives have been discovered in the glaring light of the international market's demands. Assuming that management decides there are enough positive conclusions to study the export market in detail, where and how should one begin? The inventory may have turned up some successful contracts overseas that provided designs and services needed in the developing countries. Perhaps one of the partners was born in a Latin country and has strong cultural ties, good language capability, and professional credibility. Such a person is ready to lead a mission south of the border. A word of caution: It may be a challenge to hold this individual in check until the foreign marketing plan is approved.

A task force should be organized, headed by an engineer with enough status to insist on the priorities and support for the study and with ability to organize research and resources. An assistant, probably a young professional with either a background of foreign residence and travel or a desire to learn international business, would be another excellent team member. Finally, a support person capable of dealing with the public would complete the team. Ideally the team should be located in a situation room where maps, market reports, periodicals—all the material gathered in the search—can be at hand during the preparation of the preliminary report and budget. The value of being in a place where interested and curious management can drop in for a look at the maps and a chat about the study should not be underestimated.

A simple way to start the market selection is to discover where the competition is working. This information is available by diligent research. Some library work, scanning trade periodicals such as *International Construction Week* newsletter or trade papers such as *Engineering News Record, Middle East Economic Digest, The Wall Street Journal, The Economist, Business America,* and *Development Forum,* will yield the data required. It is important not to go back more than a year or so, because of rapid changes in markets. One excellent source for tracking the competition is the international summary normally located at the end of *Engineering News-Record*'s annual listing of the top 500 design firms. Identify five or ten firms that might be your competitors, and list the countries where they worked last year. When clusters appear, something is happening. If it is not common knowledge, the projects these firms are working on can be tracked in the periodicals listed above or by inquiries of governmental trade offices, such as the U.S. Department of Commerce desk officer for the country in question.

While researchers are engaged in locating the competition, a quick review of the trade papers will pinpoint the more active markets. Another excellent source is the annual "Outlook" issue of *Worldwide Projects,* generally published in October. A review of the 1983 and 1984 "Outlooks" will provide an amazing amount of information, including schematic city maps and telephone numbers, addresses, and names of officials in the "hot" market areas.

This research will open a paper chase which must be controlled judiciously, or it will become confusing and overwhelming. International commercial banks publish economic reports on countries and areas where they have branches and correspondents. Chase Manhattan has excellent reports on the Middle East; Marine Midland covers the Far East well; and Latin America is well studied by a number of banks, including Citibank of New York. The international office of your own bank would like to have your foreign business and will be a good resource for market information. If your local bank does not have international experience, it will have a correspondent relationship with one or more of the big banks that does have an international department. A letter of introduction will open many doors.

Here's a parenthetical reminder: Advice from bankers can be very helpful if you seek foreign markets. Bankers tend to be more conservative and frank than our government representatives, and their information comes from outspoken sources. When the stakes are large, a word from the president of your firm to the head of the bank may reveal facts that will not be available in print for weeks, if ever.

Having located where the competition is working, determined the economic conditions in these countries, and identified the countries which look like future prospects, it is time to check out the economic and political risks. When several wars are under way at once, as happened in the early 1980s, the risks are obvious. For the purpose of the market study, it will suffice to sample some typical reports that rate political turmoil as well as financial, manufacturing, and export risk. Some of these risk-analysis reports may awaken thoughts that will interfere with one's normal sleep patterns. But they are very useful in dealing with top management when it seeks your opinion about certain markets. There is enough risk in the engineering business under normal conditions, without opening an office in a battle zone.

In addition to risk-analysis reports a number of consultants are available for advice on political and security risks. These resources include retired State Department or intelligence community personnel, highly respected professionals who are more in tune with the problems of airlines, oil companies, and bankers than the lesser affairs of engineers, architects, and construction managers. At this stage in the market study, there is no need to be concerned with such experts, except to know that they exist. When it is time to plan operations, however, such consulting may be very desirable.

By now the situation room is becoming cluttered with paper. It is time to settle on some country targets and to further narrow the selection to one or two of the most likely countries to investigate in person. In spite of several weeks of completed research, it is now worthwhile to open new sources of information. In the United States, the Department of Commerce has several services to assist firms in major international business transactions, and the best approach to this resource is through the Commerce Field Office in the nearest large city, where government publications, which will be discussed in this chapter, can be obtained. The U.S. Department of Commerce also organizes seminars on international business, and American firms should make it a point to be on its mailing list for notices of such meetings. The Office of Major Projects and the country desk officers in Washington will be an important source of information, and contact should be made with them through the nearest field office. During the homework phase a visit should be made to the field office and to the Department of Commerce in order to establish your firm's potential interest and to pick up information available from government sources about the target countries. The effort, if well planned, should take two full days in Washington. Besides telling the dedicated professional trade specialists about your goals in this homework phase, you should obtain the following items from the Department of Commerce or the U.S. Government Printing Office store in the same building:

1. *The Area Handbooks.* Everything you need to know about the target countries. Prepared for the Department of Defense by American University, these books cover geography, history, politics, culture, economy, industry, agriculture, and many other features.

2. *Foreign Economic Trend Reports (FET).* An update on the economic outlook prepared by the U.S. Embassy.

3. *Overseas Business Reports (OBR).* Marketing guides that are quite comprehensive (dealing with the best prospects for U.S. exporters) contain the departments' assessment of the market, and have a wealth of details not found in any other single source.

4. *State Department Background Notes.* A very brief summary of the major items covered in the area handbooks in item 1.

In addition to these standard items, the Department of Commerce publishes many books, reports, and a monthly trade journal, *Business America,* which will be of great value when entering the foreign market.

Department of Commerce desk officers are the link to the department's trade specialists in foreign countries, and they are usually quite knowledgeable about local conditions. Many have served in the country they now deal with and, consequently, can be helpful in very practical ways. Frequently, desk officers have single copies of special reports on the engineering and construction sector and on other areas of interest which they will lend for a short period while a copy can be made.

The Office of Major Projects is the source of information about potential construction or purchase contracts overseas with substantial export content (at least $5 million), and through it the U.S. government provides a significant service to American exporters. "Major Projects" is continually striving to provide early and complete information to architects and engineers. If informed of specific fields and geographic areas of interest, trade specialists will include your firm on the list to receive copies of messages from their field staff and other news about programs and foreign government plans. This service is free and open to all interested firms, but frequently it is not timely. Since the Department of Commerce reflects the attitude of the federal government, the level of its support may not be constant over several administrations. Department of Commerce personnel, in common with other bureaucrats, provide varying degrees of help, but their service to the design professions is generally outstanding. Frequent visits, sharing of information, and acknowledgment in writing of specific cases in which you were helped by a department member will produce the best results and promote good relations.

Many other information sources will provide background about target countries. In fact, there are so many that control must be used to stay on the path to the goal without diversion. Information by itself is worthless if it cannot be digested and used effectively in building a profitable export business. The following may be valuable in providing scarce background material:

- Country handbooks on tax and financial matters from the major international accounting firms can be very useful. Ernst and Whinney and Price Waterhouse, in particular, publish excellent material.
- Major national airlines publish helpful guides to business in their own countries and those they serve. KLM has an excellent handbook on the Middle East.
- The American Chamber of Commerce, whose members operate overseas, is a good source of material about business conditions in specific countries.

- National Geographic, Washington, D.C., is the best source of maps.

- American Management Association (AMA), 135 West 50th Street, New York, NY 10020, conducts seminars, publishes briefing papers and other material about foreign operations, export marketing, and international trade. Although the AMA is oriented toward major industries and manufacturers, its material about cross-cultural relations and the development of management personnel for international operations is outstanding.

Some of the information services are quite expensive, and it will be logical and necessary to budget this item carefully. It is easy to spend $5000 annually (1984 prices) for a modest number of commercially produced reports and periodicals. Each information source should be evaluated as to reliability, scope, and timeliness.

If your firm's entry into the export market is to be a success, the materials should be carefully selected and filed. During the homework stage a very simple filing system can be started using ring-binder notebooks for each country, which will grow into valuable references for your international staff. Their initial cost will be very reasonable compared with outside research. Moreover, their content will be focused toward your specific corporate interests. These notebooks will save valuable time for top management and will be of great help when you are trying to gain the commitment of the board of directors. Finally, the notebooks will be excellent for briefing employees and their families who are later assigned to overseas projects.

A typical notebook index illustrates what might be included (from a Gabon notebook—1976 CLL):

1. Maps—continent, country, and major cities.
2. *Traveller's Africa* (Gabon Section—Tourist Guide).
3. State Department Background Notes—Gabon.
4. "Gabon"—from AFRICA 74/75, *Economist* special report.
5. "Development in Gabon"—*Swiss Review of World Affairs.*
6. Guide for American Business Visitors (Airgram—U.S. Embassy).
7. American Companies Represented in Gabon (Airgram—U.S. Embassy).

8. American Businessmen's Association (Airgram—U.S. Embassy).
9. Composition of Government of Gabon Cabinet (Airgram—U.S. Embassy).
10. *Economic Trends Report for Gabon* (U.S. Department of Commerce).
11. Overseas Business Reports—*Marketing in Gabon* (U.S. Department of Commerce).
12. Gabonese Budget for 1976 (Airgram—U.S. Embassy).
13. Voluntary Best Prospects Report for Gabon (Airgram—U.S. Embassy).
14. Gabonese Investment Law of 1967.
15. Summary of Tax System 1976.
16. Newspaper clippings from *New York Times, Christian Science Monitor, Wall Street Journal.*
17. "Gabon's Increased Revenues Hasten Work on Trans-Gabon Railway"—IMF Survey June 7, 1976.
18. Speech by President Bengo—May 1976—"Rapid Economic Development Boosted by Oil."
19. Visa and flight information—from ABC Airways Guide.

The notebook you produce for your first target country might follow such a format. The sole test is that it be easy to use, relatively inexpensive to assemble, and accessible to all concerned. The production of country notebooks can be handled by a marketing assistant using sources similar to those described above.

Now the task at hand is to study the information collected, then to select the most attractive target country and start the preliminary report to management. The choices should be narrowed to three to four countries, preferably in different parts of the world. One country and one alternate should be selected, then a case made for the number-one choice. The fact-finding trip, even for old hands, should be confined to one country at a time. If not, the team will get an overdose of travel and of new culture—and will risk becoming frustrated. This condition may result in an urge to return home before the mission is completed. Even if the trip includes only one country, it may be necessary to go back again before the final report is completed and management is convinced that it should proceed with the marketing plan.

During the homework period, listing the strengths and

weaknesses of the firm revealed several countries where the firm's personnel had some individual experience. It also uncovered three or four countries whose development plans indicated infrastructure projects very similar to contracts recently completed by the firm—for example, a mass-housing project for employees of an oil company which was a present client; a vocational training school with boarding facilities, similar to one designed for a Southwest Indian community; and a traffic study for a sprawling city in the Arab Gulf. All these projects would have been attractive. The test will be to determine whether the firm could operate successfully in these countries, make a profit, and do a good job. That is what the fact-finding trip is all about. It is not intended to be a marketing trip. The goal will be to gather enough facts and cost data to decide whether to make a marketing effort in the target country and to develop a budget for the first year.

Not more than three people should make the fact-finding trip. Travel costs are high, and the task is better done by individuals than a committee. The travel plan should be arranged not to conflict with local holidays, vacation periods, or a known season of bad weather. The schedule should allow at least one but not more than two weeks in a target country. More than ten working days can create confusion; less than two weeks will not allow enough time to arrange a formal appointment schedule.

The following is an example of a typical budget for a fact-finding trip to the Middle East for three people (1984 prices). It assumes that a U.S. east coast departure will be made and that the team will include two $60,000-per-year company officers and one $40,000-per-year senior engineer. Their hourly rates are $28.74 and $19.16, respectively, based on 2088 hours per year, with a daily team salary of $613.12 (rounded to $614).

## Direct Costs

1. Air fares (business class)
   (3 × $2586)                                                    $ 7758
2. Preparation expense—visas, passports, photos, shots, medicine, presents, special brochures, powers of attorney                              1500
3. Hotel and meals ($200 per day × 12 days × 3 persons)                                                            7200

| | | |
|---|---|---:|
| **4.** | Car rental and taxis | 1000 |
| **5.** | Entertainment | 500 |
| **6.** | Telex and telephone | 1000 |
| **7.** | Translators and interpreters | 1000 |
| **8.** | Contingency (15%) | 2994 |
| | *Subtotal direct costs* | $22,952 |

**Labor**

| | | |
|---|---|---:|
| **1.** | Pretrip preparation (3 days × $640) | $ 1920 |
| **2.** | Actual trip time (14 days × $640) | 8960 |
| **3.** | Debriefing and report (3 days minimum) | 1920 |
| **4.** | Secretarial and graphics support for report | 1200 |
| **5.** | General and salary related overhead at 100% of labor | 14,000 |
| | *Subtotal labor* | 28,000 |
| | *Total budgeted cost of trip (say $51,000)* | $50,952 |

The labor cost should be computed in accordance with your firm's policy. But to be realistic, it should include salary-related overheads and general overheads at rates normally charged other marketing efforts for technical personnel.

If the trip crosses more than five time zones, a one-day stopover should be programmed so team members arrive on the scene in good physical condition. A stopover should also be programmed on the return to allow the team to collect their thoughts, put some perspective to the trip, and perhaps outline final conclusions and recommendations.

It is sound business to put up the team in a four- or five-star hotel. Not only will it be comfortable, but its communications will probably be dependable for keeping in touch with the home office. Moreover, the team's local contacts will be impressed, not shocked, by the firm's choice of lodging, and the hotel will be an acceptable place for business entertainment. After the first contract is awarded, more economical arrangements may be considered.

The airline tickets should be valid for a year, to allow changes in route and switching of carriers, if necessary. No economy on this item, either, is justified for the fact-finding trip.

A brief presentation should be very carefully presented to top management before departure, to get budget approval. More important, it will promote real understanding of the reasons for the trip and the expected goals. The purposes of the trip are to determine the firm's ability to operate profitably in the target country, to decide if it is worthwhile to initiate a marketing program there, and to develop a budget for the first year's marketing effort. The planned purposes of the trip should be made clear to all. Otherwise the team members will be badgered by everyone from the chairperson to the company driver, on return, asking (with a smirk), "What kind of a job did you bring back for us?" It would be a miracle if this team returned with a contract—or even a request for a proposal. Life is not like that, although some may remember when the firm's founder signed up a bridge design contract in the lounge of a PanAm clipper on a flight to Africa.

The fact-finding trip is a difficult and crucial step and is as far as many firms get into the export market. The next chapter will be devoted to that important event.

# CHAPTER 3

# THE
# FACT-FINDING TRIP

After some weeks of homework, impatience and boredom will inevitably strike. Why waste time on homework when we could be out there competing and getting contracts? During further discussions of international operations, this objection will be voiced repeatedly. The proposition of organizing a small international unit, preparing its own detailed plan and approved budget, and winning a strong corporate commitment should be well understood. Exporting professional services in this rapidly changing world is not a simple task. The success rate for new entrants in the international market is low. Hard data are not available, but based on my personal knowledge gathered during forty years of experience, it seems reasonable to assume that failures outnumber successes by a ratio of 5 to 1.

From 1963 to 1975 in Europe, Africa, and the Middle East, U.S. firms flashed across the scene like meteors across the sky. Of the dozens of firms attempting to enter this once very lucrative market, less than ten stayed in the arena for ten years. The reasons for the withdrawal from the market—if not failure— were many and varied. The loss of money, spirit, and interest by well-intentioned individuals and their companies was appalling.

The conclusion is that the international design and construction market is a treacherous one which offers rewards and risks equally. Entry into the market must be planned as one would confront a complex engineering problem. The firms that have succeeded are amazingly similar in their studied approach. Although one might rush out from a board meeting, buy the tickets, fly to Saudi Arabia, sign the first contract, and be home by the weekend, the odds are against it. Obviously one would not refuse a profitable contract on the first business trip abroad. But until the opportunity is identified, the fact-finding mission must be conducted with only a few basic goals in mind.

The target country having been chosen, an area notebook produced and studied, and management having approved a budget for the trip, the mission's goals are:

- Obtain cost data for launching a marketing effort.
- Evaluate the need for local associates and start the search for candidates.
- Verify economic and political risks.
- Identify an acceptable bank.
- Advise the U.S. embassy's foreign commercial service officer of plans to enter the market, and find out what, if any, support is available from this source.
- Obtain an impression of the firm's ability to operate successfully under local conditions.
- Present a report to management.

An action plan should be developed, assigning priorities, responsibilities, and individual tasks to the team members. It will save time and avoid confusion if one person with some international travel experience is given responsibility for logistics. Efforts could start immediately with the following:

| | |
|---|---|
| Airline reservations and tickets | Brochures |
| | Passports and visas |
| Special medicines | Tape recorders |
| Hotel bookings | Immunizations |
| Letters of introduction | Stationery and supplies |
| Rental cars | |

The team leader should assign general responsibilities to each member so that all the mission's goals are completed. One team member should be assigned the task of cataloging the material collected on the trip and packing it for the return flight. There is no reason for committee action on any item except opinions about the firm's ability to operate successfully under local conditions. Efficiency will be increased if the team splits up after the first day or so, with each person accomplishing assigned tasks. As a group the team might call on the U.S. embassy (bureaucrats are impressed by numbers) and on potential associates. A consensus is useful when evaluating these items. But for other objectives valuable time will be saved by individual action.

Cost-of-living figures can be obtained from business contacts in the country, but it is more satisfactory to get the data at the source. Apartment rental costs are most difficult to ascertain and are subject to individual taste. Some employees may demand to live on a high standard, with a swimming pool and other amenities. Food costs are easy to obtain, as is the cost of utilities and transportation. It is often helpful to subcontract this cost-gathering task to an expatriate dependent who can use contacts without appearing to be the representative of a rich, impersonal corporation. It is recommended that cost-of-living data be collected from the very first day so all team members have the opportunity to verify main items and any others that particularly interest them. No credibility should be given to an *embassy post report*, which is compiled to make every foreign city look like a hardship area.

Checklists of questions should be compiled in connection with the firm's lawyers, accountants, and bankers for use in identifying legal, accounting, and banking services in the target country. Such discussions may simplify the search, because many U.S. banks, for example, will have a correspondent relationship with one or more principal banks in a strong export market area, as will international accounting and law firms. The team's task will be reduced to determining whether the correspondent has a good reputation and whether the staff is compatible.

The Department of Commerce country desk officer in Washington may have a list of local firms that have indicated to the U.S. embassy that they would like to associate with a U.S. engineering or architectural firm. In any case, the desk officer could advise the embassy that your team will be on the scene and will interview prospective associates during the visit. It would be worthwhile to discuss the matter with the desk officer because there may be no likely associates available or all the acceptable ones may already be committed.

When the action plan is sketched out—at least a week before arrival in the target country—messages should be telexed advising prospective contacts of the team's impending visit, the length of stay, the purpose of the visit to them, and that, once in the country, a call will be made to arrange an appointment. This last point is a subtle, though simple, one. People from other cultures are not as quick to set firm appointments with strangers as we are at home, and may take offense at being given what they may consider an ultimatum. So, on the first day in the target country, make appointments on the home team's schedule and rearrange your program to fit.

On arrival in the target country, the leader might telex the home office, to notify concerned individuals of the telephone numbers, hotel room numbers, and the time differential. This information will obviously improve communications and is worthwhile because during the first trip there will be a need for consultation. More important, it is essential to demonstrate to management the relative ease (or difficulty) of communicating with the home office. Foreign opportunities have been turned down by management because of difficult communications, and one of the purposes of this trip is to check out all facilities.

The goals of the fact-finding trip are simple. The leader's major task will be to keep the team on track. Diversions will come from all sides—some good, many time-wasting. A certain amount of time should be spent learning about the new culture and getting acquainted with potential associates. As representatives of a well-known international consulting firm, your opinion may be sought on everything from selecting a university for a child of a newfound friend to the location of an irrigation dam. Resist trips to the interior and social invitations. Avoid getting sidetracked by problems which have no relationship to the goals of the mission.

Another possible diversion may come when an opportunity is offered, such as a request for proposal for services on a large project which profiles well with the strengths of the firm. If, at first inspection of the written scope of work, the opportunity looks real, the job is financed, and there is sufficient time to prepare a detailed proposal back at the home office, the team leader should make a decision. The efforts of the fact-finding team should not be abandoned. It is very doubtful that one would not have learned of a good opportunity before leaving home because legitimate, financed projects are well advertised. If more help is needed, it should be summoned from home after consultation with management.

Assuming that the trip will last two working weeks, the team will be ready for two days of rest and recreation on the weekend. It is important that the team be alert, so this rest period should be protected. A progress review should be held on the weekend to check missing or unavailable information and to plan the final week's schedule. If the mission has gone well, most of the information collected in the field will verify the results of the homework. There will be some new factors, such as changes in government, new development plans, and other predictable changes. The area of fact-finding which is most difficult is the roster of potential associates. There never seems to be enough time to address this task properly. In fact, an entire later chapter will be devoted to this subject and to final selection. It will be a challenge to locate a good firm, respected professionally, politically acceptable, and without restrictive ties to other foreign consultants. If the country is small, there may be only a few professionals, and they may not wish to form exclusive associations. In another typical circumstance, all reputable firms may be committed to long-term associations. This points to a need to talk to as many candidates as possible— three or more—to develop a basis for comparison. It could be that you will have to "sell" management to the local organization. Be prepared to adapt to the situation as it presents itself. It is prudent to get as much information as possible, maintaining a friendly but noncommittal posture. The time for evaluation and decisions comes after your firm has accepted the fact-finding report and confirmed its commitment to enter the market.

After some ten days of hectic, enjoyable, and challenging pavement pounding, the final two days of effort must be planned. Departure conferences should be scheduled with the important people. Not the lawyers, accountants, bankers, or real estate agents—they will be there when you return. But formal good-byes should be said to any local government officials who have been sympathetic; to the ambassador, if you got an audience, or to the commercial service officer; and, finally, to any particularly attractive candidate for association. It is important that the leader make these calls, with or without the team. All the above-mentioned people respect organizational status; consequently, one should leave some well-defined tracks in the new territory, so that a presence is felt. This will make the next trip much easier and will facilitate telephone conversations when you return to the home office. A little "old world charm" becomes very useful at this time.

As a final step before you leave for home, the collected data should be rechecked and the missing items located or canceled. An outline of the final report should be blocked out, in preparation for the job ahead at home. The team should reserve some quiet time to discuss their ideas for the final recommendations to management. In this way a "party line" will be formulated to give to interested associates upon the team's return when any member is encountered individually in the interim period before the final report is released.

The most scrutinized item in the formal report will probably be the cost of placing a marketer in the country for a year. A format for this estimate should be established before departure, with the help of the firm's accounting and personnel departments. Before overseas allowances and tax equalization plans are established, consultation should develop what the compensation policy is with similar firms. This information can be obtained from compensation consultants and international accounting firms. These sources also have figures on the costs of living and perquisites in remote areas that should be checked in the target country. Care must be taken to learn what other firms are providing their employees, so the budget will reflect actual facts and be adequate.

My first participation in a fact-finding trip for the purpose of establishing a foreign operation came in 1955. I was happily occupied as project manager on a large expressway project in Florida, when one day the senior partner stopped me at the water fountain and said, "I understand you speak Spanish." I admitted that he understood correctly, and my quizzical expression led him to respond: "Fine, I want you to go to Panama with me tomorrow." Eventually I learned that a new corporation had been formed with the help of a Panamanian law firm and that there were indeed plans to open a representative office. I had been selected and named in the application as manager of the operation.

We went to Panama on what the senior partner called a

"fact-finding" trip—but actually the die had already been cast. The apparent goals of the trip were as follows:

1. To check the banking secrecy laws of Panama
2. To determine Panama's value as a tax haven for revenues from all foreign contracts and how to take maximum advantage of it
3. To lease suitable quarters for a representative office
4. To determine cost-of-living information, so that the senior partner could make an offer to the prospective manager for salary and perquisites for his new position

We accomplished our mission in about four days—the senior partner handling items 1 and 2, and I, items 3 and 4. I later learned that the senior partner made his own check on cost of living so that he would be in a position to negotiate my new salary and allowances. It was not a real fact-finding trip, such as has been described in this chapter. The decision had been made to establish a representative office, and it was "damn the torpedoes—full speed ahead." Not much meaningful study was done, and there was no report to be made. The senior partner arrived at decisions on hunches, gut feelings, and input from involved parties. But there was much to be learned from this senior partner. It was clear that the advice received from the most prestigious legal and accounting firms in Panama got the venture off to a good start which ultimately led to a decade or more of successful operation.

A biased view and bad impressions of a new market may result if one puts total reliance on a prospective local associate. Because this person speaks the local language and understands the culture, it may seem to be advantageous to accept proffered help. On the contrary, the candidate's reputation, political affiliations, friendships, language fluency, and enunciation may be distinct disadvantages. This has happened to me at various times in France, the Middle East, Iran, and South Africa. A clouded impression is the general result, as well as much wasted time. The local person has personal prejudices and contacts and not much knowledge of your firm's background, reputation, and operating policy. It is more revealing and satisfying to conduct an independent fact-finding mission. The associate should be selected after the market has been evaluated.

On a fact-finding mission it is often necessary to use a translator to eliminate the severe problem of language gap. Even if one has a good working knowledge of another language, it may be difficult to have meaningful business meetings without some help. If one has a good linguist on the team, even the whispered asides of the other party take on meaning. While westerners may consider it rude to speak in English in front of someone who does not understood the language well, other cultures have no such inhibitions. Frequently one may detect a remark like "What is this guy trying to say?" So when another language is involved, take along a trusted associate who speaks it fluently.

Beware the use of commercial interpreters who work on a time basis for business visitors. They are great for sightseeing but dangerous in discussions with other professionals. Often when the interpreter senses one's lack of knowledge of the language and culture, there will be no hesitancy to wade into deep water. This is particularly true in French-speaking countries, it seems, where the burden for discovering what is going on always falls on the visitor. When one discovers that the interpreter is becoming a hindrance, the best action is to end the contractual relationship and to seek help elsewhere. A local professional who speaks English may be the answer. In Guatemala we were unable to break a deadlock in discussions because of language difficulties. The senior man on the other team was very gracious, and I suggested that he might have a trusted friend who spoke English fluently. We drove for some distance to the home of a local engineer who had graduated from a California university, got him out of bed, and pressed him into service. Within an hour the problem had been resolved.

In cases of extreme frustration with language barriers one may be tempted to fall back on any available source of help. For example, in making a business call in Turkey, where a visitor probably cannot even read the street signs or building numbers, it may seem helpful to enlist the taxi driver's help just because he understands English. The local businessperson, who was brought up on ideas of "face" and status, however, will not be amused if someone like this is introduced into a meeting.

Successful fact-finding missions with two or three team members have been made in Greece, Libya, Ireland, Iran, Cyprus, South Africa, Nigeria, India, and Mexico. That is to say the fact-finding missions were accomplished, although in some cases a negative decision concerning operations resulted. And of course good negative decisions are just as important as good positive ones. Fortunately, with the existence of good background information and homework on the target country, there is not as much probability as there was twenty years ago that a negative report will be the result. Some of the missions mentioned above could have been eliminated if there had been proper background information for an in-depth study at home. Even in more enlightened times, a proposed fact-finding trip may be based on a whim of a board member or senior partner who has some connection with a new market area. For such a mission the team has the sad duty of bringing back the bad news that the market is not promising and that an operation there will be a bad investment. Sometimes this happens in garden spots like Malta, Cyprus, Bermuda, or Costa Rica, where there is just not enough business to support another international architectural and engineering operation. It should be possible, however, with the facilities and information available, to eliminate these frivolous market suggestions without leaving home.

The final report on the fact-finding trip should be concise, explicit, and factual. There should be a one-page executive summary. The end product should be a recommendation to go or not go, with estimates of the cost of marketing and of making a given number of proposals and a draft marketing plan. The scenario for selecting an associate should be set forth, with perhaps a short list of candidates. Finally, the budget should include a conservative item for contingencies, because there will be some. The presentation of the report should be made by the team leader. This person's contagious enthusiasm or lack of it, as a result of the fact-finding trip, will be a large factor in the management decision to export.

The following principles should govern the fact-finding trip:

- Define the goals of fact-finding trip and make certain team members and management understand them.
- Make an action plan and stick to it.
- Assign trip logistics to a detail-oriented professional.
- Assign trip responsibilities during the planning period.
- Compile checklists with the help of lawyers, bankers, and accountants.

- Make maximum use of the U.S. Department of Commerce facilities.
- Advise intended contacts of your schedule in the target country.
- Don't get diverted by fiestas and sightseeing.
- Regroup and rest at midpoint in the fact-finding visit.
- Prepare to cope with the language barrier. Beware commercial interpreters.
- The final report and budget should be clear, concise, and factual.
- Present the report to management with enthusiasm and confidence.

# CHAPTER 4

# COMMITMENT, THE MAGIC ELEMENT

There are many unknowns and indeterminate factors affecting business relationships in the international field, which are not encountered in domestic practice. The challenges of learning a new language, adapting to another culture, managing an unstable currency, or living in a hostile environment are shocking to many. In almost every phase of a foreign operation there are obstacles for the unprepared. Professional training and intelligence are not enough—perseverance, patience, and commitment are also needed to export services successfully.

Until entering the international scene, a dedicated professional may never have given serious consideration to the need to be committed. Steady progression up the organizational ladder may have come as a result of hard work and intelligence, without special dedication or zeal. But now the need for yet another virtue suddenly arises. Why? What is commitment, and why do we talk about it?

In engineering education, the psychological requirements of the profession are usually assumed or ignored. Emphasis is generally placed on role models who were leaders in the technical aspects of the profession. Little mention is made of those individuals who directed multinational design and construction efforts. To build a Panama Canal, an Alaska pipeline, a Mont Blanc Tunnel, or a Yanbu city, committed professionals were needed. In a similar way the development of the petroleum industry and its accompanying infrastructure in the Middle East has depended on committed professionals.

Commitment is defined as a pledge or a promise, which is generally related to the legal and medical professions. But now we are saying that a design and construction management professional needs this elusive element in the international marketplace. It is a fact that the firms which have been successful on international projects seem to have dedicated employees and committed management. In this sense, commitment means being tenacious enough to stay on the job through all sorts of unfavorable events and conditions and to deliver a completed project.

In addition to a corporate image of being pledged to the export market, some individuals managing international operations have an almost passionate devotion to foreign trade. The committed firm is easily recognized by experienced exporters because of the telltale signs that identify both firm and employees. To identify good potential joint-venture partners who will adapt well to international operations, look for the following vital clues:

## Organizations

- Although the home office of a successful exporter can be anywhere, a location near an international airport or export center is a very positive sign.
- Exporters tend to have active offshore subsidiaries.
- A committed international firm will have language capabilities on its staff and, usually, a number of foreign-born employees in its international department.
- World maps and clocks indicating the time in principal market areas will be in a prominent place. The offices tend to be decorated with foreign art.
- Telex machines will be located convenient to management, not hidden away in the mail room.
- The fact that a firm has completed several contracts abroad does not always signify success or commitment. Dig deeper.

- A truly committed firm will have made arrangements for legal, accounting, and banking help in a new export market before starting the fact-finding trip.

## Individuals

- The successful exporter likes to travel and *always* has a valid passport.
- Committed internationalists do not regale visitors with stories of hardships, lost baggage, and rough flights on foreign airlines.
- While two-career and immobile families are increasing in number, a good candidate for a foreign post will have considered family situations before showing interest in a foreign assignment.
- A good potential foreign employee will already have become familiar with foreign cultures and *have* learned another language. (The person who expects to learn a new language in eight weeks by immersion will be a liability.)

It is not easy to identify misfit firms and individuals in the international field, because there are no hard-and-fast rules or criteria. On the other hand, it is not difficult to pick out the capable exporters, who seem to go about their business with ease, style, and lack of fanfare. In a recent radio interview, well-known foreign correspondent Georgie Ann Geyer stated that successful diplomats, missionaries, foreign correspondents, and international businesspeople seem to have much in common. They are identified by a drive that takes them willingly to remote places to carry out difficult missions. Design professionals who will succeed abroad fit this pattern.

In examining our own capabilities, or those of prospective joint-venture partners, what happens if we cannot identify commitment to international work? The best advice in that event is to abandon the idea, for it is wishful to think that a domestically oriented firm can adapt well to a foreign market just by association with a strong exporter. There are case histories of groups organized by engineering firms, with experience abroad, that contained those who had never been overseas. Typically, these groups begin to unravel when required to identify key personnel for foreign assignments. Result: Money, time, credibility, and contracts are wasted as one of the experienced international firms is forced to take over the contract, furnish all key people, and even assume the losses of the joint venture.

Another sign of weakness that could lead to serious financial loss is evident when top positions in the prospective foreign partner's firm are filled with incompetent domestic employees. These are people who, unsuccessful at home, are still well "protected" by their firm. They will go abroad because there is no longer a place for them in the domestic organization. Their failure abroad will often come as a surprise after the damage is done. Placement of such candidates in a marketing position in a remote area can sink a good international program—half a million dollars later, with no prospects and no sales, the only rational solution will be to cut losses and close shop.

If no corporate or individual commitments are found when assessing the international capabilities of an organization, what then? There are several ways of stimulating corporate and personnel interest and enthusiasm—given the backing of the board of directors and the CEO. Sometimes, and despite weak support, a reluctant board's attitude can be turned around. Usually the road to profitable foreign operations is long, and the foreign division's profitability frequently difficult to prove because of inequitable distribution of corporate overhead. Commitment can be built by bringing in, at officer or partner level, a person with a proven international record to head the effort. With proper backing and incentives, international operations can succeed when managed by an experienced newcomer.

Participation in seminars and in international activities of professional societies will not only build commitment but also provide information and contacts that help strengthen the international division. The American Management Association sponsors seminars on international business, meetings which offer good exposure to excellent background and opportunities to meet export-oriented people. The cost of attending such seminars is high, and the material is oriented toward managers, but among the greatest benefits is an exposure to the literature of export and to professionals in many fields, such as lawyers and accountants. The seminar speakers are usually marketing their services or looking for joint-venture partners, and this can make the programs especially interesting and useful to organizations entering the market.

langingNT, THE MAGIC ELEMENT**   **31**

The American Consulting Engineer's Council has an International Engineering Committee (ICE) composed of representatives of export-minded firms. The ICE meets about four times each year, providing a forum for the interchange of ideas and liaison with export-oriented U.S. government agencies. Membership provides opportunities for learning what's happening in the market.

Another way to develop interest, enthusiasm, and involvement in international trade is to send one of the firm's top management on a government-sponsored trade mission. Tours of promising market areas are scheduled several times yearly by the U.S. Department of Commerce, which selects tour members from interested design firms. Some care is taken to choose organizations in noncompeting fields, who pay their own expenses and for the cost of conducting seminars and receptions in the host countries. The Department of Commerce organizes the tour and the meetings. Industry usually provides an experienced leader. The mission promotes the export of professional services at seminars arranged with host government and industry users of such services. Members of the mission give technical presentations in their fields and have, as well, some time to meet prospective clients. In my opinion, these trade missions are an excellent opportunity for professionals without previous international marketing experience. The members are spoonfed in an almost laboratory atmosphere and exposed to the real world by experienced guides. Such trade missions indoctrinate already competent yet domestically oriented persons. They eliminate some of the loneliness, chaos, and frustration that otherwise might be encountered on a solo performance in a strange country. Although there is only a small chance of a member of the mission landing a contract on these short visits, many good contacts have been made which resulted in return calls with sales. Attendance at a trade mission is an excellent method of developing the enthusiasm of a senior member of your firm. The resulting publicity is an ego tonic, and after returning home, the individual is an instant "international expert" among colleagues at management meetings. This is good for building commitment.

The magic ingredient is commitment. It is something that cannot be learned from books. Perhaps commitment can be learned by on-the-job training. At any rate, an international engineering firm without enthusiasm, awareness, and style in the foreign market is doomed to mediocrity or failure. In this chapter, suggestions were made for identifying the necessary elements and methods for developing commitment in individuals and divisions. If your team doesn't have the stuff, get some new players, review the fundamentals, and try to build a winner in the export market.

# CHAPTER 5

# SELECTING
# AN ASSOCIATE

In the recent past—before energy shortages, perhaps—selecting a local "partner" in the third world was simple. There were usually no architects or engineers available in the project country. If they did exist, they probably occupied high ministry positions.

In this atmosphere the foreign consultant had to join with a commercial agent—just like the shipping companies and the automakers. The agent viewed the role as a consultant's associate in the same light as work with an international shipping company: Making hotel reservations, meeting planes, getting appointments, and acting as guide, translator, interpreter, and guardian were the primary responsibilities.

Generally speaking, *influence*—real or imagined—was thought to justify the balance of the agent's fee (the part not earned by the foregoing activities) paid by the consultant with great reluctance, at long intervals. "He gets his after I get mine" was the watchword. When the scope of work of the design was discussed, the local person was usually excluded, or dismissed from the meeting, since everyone knew a "local" couldn't contribute anything.

In the past five years, "the winds of change" have truly been blowing. The imperialistic approach has all but disappeared. The foreign consultant has gone from being in a commanding position to being a partner with a local firm, and often a minority one at that. It is no longer necessary to apologize to the home office for such liaisons. Local professionals are following the practice of those in more developed countries, establishing societies to solidify their ranks and to bring their points of view to the attention of their governments. These newly formed consulting engineering organizations represent an educated and sophisticated segment of society and make up a significant number of a rapidly developing country's educated citizens. Their governments are responding to their demands for recognition as are international development agencies.

In Latin America, Africa, and now in the wealthier Middle East (Kuwait, Saudi Arabia, and the Persian Gulf States), local professionals are loath to make lasting commitments to any one foreign consulting engineer. They feel that when a project of a different nature comes along, they might find a more prestigious and qualified expatriate firm as their associate. A short time ago I was in the office of a foreign associate, working on a joint proposal. In three days he received three separate invitations by telephone to associate with foreign consultants on other projects.

I couldn't blame the local man for feeling confident about his power to choose! In these countries, a knowledgeable foreign consultant will make an early choice and cover handshakes with a joint letter of intent to associate. Associations, then, are in vogue, both for the strong and the weak, in the busy rapidly developing countries.

The art of finding a local partner has become more complex and sophisticated as the need for such help has increased. Eventually, when it finally dawned on the traveling partner that help was needed, all suggestions were entertained, whether they came from the occupant of the next stool at the Hilton bar in Athens, from the manager of the Scheherazade Restaurant, or the ambassador's spouse. Candidates selected in this random fashion had a high spoilage rate. It was not unusual to wear out three or four associates on a good-sized job, until one was found who suited both consultant and client.

Consider the actual cases of how such local partners have been chosen that follow, and marvel at the possibility that any of them proved useful!

- Consultants known to be interested in international projects attract shady characters as a magnet draws bits of metal. Such people often allege that they hold the secret to a huge project in an unknown country, the name of which they will divulge along with the name of a local associate when advanced a lump sum of front-end money. Chances are excellent there is no such job; it has already been built; or it is not viable. Once payment is made, the culprit disappears, and the local associate, if locatable, turns out to be a shady character.

- A local engineer identifies a foreign consultant in the directory pages of a professional magazine and makes contact, suggesting association for a project in the person's home country. This is a perfectly ethical way to find a local partner, but a successful liaison may not result. By the time the two parties find out they are not compatible, the job has gone to a more aggressive professional.

- The client assures the consultant that his firm has been selected for the big highway design project but complains that the consultant has no local associate. But he is not to worry, the minister's brother-in-law is a very competent engineer with a small staff of moonlighting government employees. (Perhaps they're the same people who will review the consultant's design!) This potential associate probably intends to "play dead" after receiving an advance on his fee, and the entire setup reeks of conflict of interest.

- An introduction to a "very competent local associate" will be provided by a "western legal consultant" who has a good working knowledge of how things are done in Iran, Lebanon, or Libya. This legal consultant is more of a "fixer" than a real legal adviser. The fee for that introduction could very well be a year's retainer, for which the legal consultant declines to do anything. The local associate may or may not work out, but the fixer gets a fee regardless.

These methods are only a few that have been employed in local partner selection, and as can be imagined, the failure rate is high.

There is a more rational way to select a local associate, and it is disgustingly simple, tedious, and time-consuming. The selection process requires hard work under trying conditions and probably larger measures of perseverance than brilliance.

If you seek alternate methods, the only one I can recommend is one given to me by a friend. When describing the utter incompetence of a local partner, he said, "I could have picked a better man. If I had thrown a dart at a list of ten names, I would have hit a smarter partner."

First, the search must be conducted in the project country. This will eliminate the unfit and unworthy candidates, such as relatives of your employees, relatives of foreign embassy personnel, or engineering students studying in your country. It is important to see any future partners in their own habitat, so they can be judged firsthand and in comparison with their peers.

The search should be organized in a logical sequence, in the same manner that the problems of plant site location or a feasibility study for a sewer system might be undertaken. It would be a helpful guide if you were to write down a simple description of the tasks to be performed by the local partner and to define what the person should ideally bring to the union. If the arrangement is to be permanent, for an indefinite time, and for a number of projects, the task will be more difficult than looking for a one-project partner.

In the latter case, the partner you want probably knows more about the project than you do, and the search boils down to either finding someone who has not already agreed on a foreign liaison or awakening an interest in an otherwise qualified person who had decided not to compete. But whether one is searching for a single person or a firm, I regard both cases as the problem of identifying an individual. If the chief executive officer of a local firm turns out to be a capable professional with a good reputation, chances are that you have found a good associate, and the staff will live up to its responsibilities and agreements.

First, there is a certain amount of homework to be accomplished before the trip is planned, of course. Besides background about the country, the foreign consultant should know the state of the engineering profession, the existence and influence of professional societies, and the professional and commercial registration requirements. It's not hard to find names of local companies associating with foreign firms on big projects. It is rarely worthwhile to contact foreign embassies in your home country about projects, consulting firms, or individual professionals in their home country. The embassy, after all, is charged with the task of handling its political relations with your country, and except for the harried commercial officer, its staff has no reason to know your field. And there's always the possibility that any contact made with a foreign embassy will provide introductions to relatives who will make a "great local associate." This type of help is guaranteed to produce chaos.

When taking the search abroad, plan enough time to get the job done right. Indeed, a first visit may result in only a short list of candidates. Several trips may be necessary to get an agreement of association and to work out details of a permanent liaison or even the definition of responsibility for given project tasks. The following items pertinent to your task could be sought:

- A list of consultants and architects
- Addresses of professional societies and names of their executive secretaries
- Names of foreign firms doing business in the host country and names of their local associates (who probably are not interested in taking on more partners)
- Names of any local professionals or firms who have expressed a desire to represent or contact foreign architects or engineers
- Finally, the U.S. Embassy commercial officer's own opinion and recommendations

Business in most parts of the world is conducted in complete secrecy—and this includes secrecy from partners, employees, and families as well as from competitors. An idea of a company's credit standing may be obtained from officers of the leading banks, particularly from those of American or British institutions.

I have had two notable failures in searching for credit information with local banks. I once asked an Italian bank (one of the world's largest) for a confidential credit report on a flamboyant Italian contractor who was dodging explicit questions about his financial capacity to undertake a large project. It turned out the contractor was a board member of the bank, and he didn't like the idea, to say the least. The other case concerned a discreet request to a Saudi bank about the creditworthiness and general reputation of a certain person who turned out to be a valued client of that bank. Glowing reports came forth (a big depositor in Saudi Arabia is a big depositor anywhere). No useful information, however, was learned about the individual's business reputation; everything was clouded by his client status.

The best one can expect is a consensus about a potential local partner. That takes time and patience. Lawyers and accountants, particularly those affiliated with international firms, are an information source, as are the resident managers of international firms. In Latin America, for example, the Pan-Am manager, the manager of Intercontinental Hotel, and shipping line managers should know your prospective partner. In the Middle East, oil company management has a good line on local professionals, and if your candidate has a clean bill with its engineering department, you probably have found a good associate.

In order to get comparisons, I feel the search is not valid unless you examine a number of candidates. One could, for example, screen a list of from five or six to a short list of three from which to pick a partner. In this way a realistic comparison is made, even if you have the three poorest candidates in the country. The problem with comparing single candidates to the job description, skills, and attributes of the perfect match is that a reasonably exact facsimile doesn't exist except in your mind.

A word about visits to local engineering and architectural societies: In many countries, as a design professional you represent the enemy. The society is dedicated to keeping all the engineering and architectural design intact for its own members or, worse yet, to steering you to a liaison with a member who is politically oriented. I recall rather cavalier treatment from an architectural society in West Africa. The president completely froze when he found I was planning to associate with one of his members. In ill-concealed rage, he marched me to the window and, pointing to the skyline, said, "One look at our beautiful modern city should convince you our profession needs no help from firms such as yours." I considered a rebuttal, but wisdom prevailed, and I beat a hasty retreat

In the end, you will have to piece together your background information and then face the candidates. After all, the acid test is whether you think your firm and his can work to achieve your goals. This can only be judged by repeated exposure and a candid exchange of views. Despite a natural tendency to cut short visits abroad, you should spend time trying to learn what kind of associate you might get.

- Will you be admitted to the "back room" of the office?
- Are associates and employees presented to you, and do they have a chance to see you alone?
- Will you be shown designs in progress and have past efforts pointed out to you with pride?
- Will you be told who clients are, and how contracts are obtained?
- What kind of family does your candidate have, and how do they live?
- Does the candidate reach for the check once in a while, or are you regarded as a big spender?
- In short, would you buy a used car from the person?

If there is any doubt remaining, perhaps now is the time to measure your prospective candidate against the following list of attributes that a good associate should possess.

- Does the person have a good reputation?
- Does he have a good rapport with government and private industry decision makers?
- Is your candidate's organization large enough to provide scarce logistic support?
- Is he fluent in your language and articulate in his own?
- Do you see a potential friend who will merit your trust?

At this point, my advice is to have a departure conference with your best candidate. Reiterate what you are looking for in an associate, and discuss (again) weak areas—not identifying them as vulnerable points, however. Then it's back to the home office to restudy your impressions and to give the problem some perspective. If in the clear light of day and the absence of jet lag, you can present the candidate to your partners as the right candidate for a longtime associate, let him know your feelings, and schedule a return visit to wrap up an association agreement.

Perhaps the most convincing argument for the local associate's being selected by an exhaustive rational search would be a few examples of how not to do it, the liaisons that resulted, and a hint of the disasters that were caused:

■  The manager of an American consulting office in Europe met a local consulting engineer who suggested the formation of joint venture. The manager was impressed by the local consultant's lifestyle. Not being able to find out anything about the consultant's background, workload, ethics, or financial condition, the manager took him to the home office so the senior partners could decide on his suitability. The liaison proceeded. After a year of joint venturing, they didn't obtain any new business, and all the capital had been used to pay the salary and office costs of the local associate, who operated in high style. The manager and the senior partners each thought the other had investigated the local. In reality, no one had done so! Each was saying, "But I thought he discussed it with you."

■  The senior partner in a European consulting firm was introduced by his engineers to a Lebanese university engineering professor. After a short courtship, the professor became a salaried associate of the firm and established an office in his Beirut home, with the mission of obtaining consulting work. No business was generated, but he did talk to a lot of politicians about projects which never came to pass. The professor finally decided he could make better proposals if he used his students as drafters and took over the design of the projects in Beirut. His tenure with the American firm was ended. Results, zero—except for some hearty expenses and a year's salary lost, as well as an activity which did nothing for the name and reputation of the international design firm.

■  An American firm was introduced to a representative of a U.S. airplane manufacturer in Saudi Arabia and finally appointed the person as its commercial agent. After a short time, the U.S. firm entered a design competition and sent a team to Saudi Arabia for a presentation. The agent performed adequately, provided support and encouragement during the week's stay in Jidda. On the final day, when all entries were displayed in a public hall and the judging was about to take place, the agent was observed in animated conversation with the American firm's main European competition! The agent was also representing the other firm!

Take time to choose well. Go through the tedious drill until the short list produces an acceptable associate. If the local rules require an associate but one cannot be found, graceful withdrawal is probably the best option. Other markets can be explored while waiting.

After the local partner is selected, discuss the person's contribution to the joint operation. Plans should be made to provide the new associate with brochures and publicity material for presentation to prospective clients. It will help to invite him to your home office to meet key staff and to get familiar with your professional background. The associate needs this exposure to select projects of interest. Otherwise, be prepared for a deluge of "hot" information on battery manufacturing plants, blanket factories, and biscuit bakeries, when in reality you are looking for a port project or a national highway program to design.

A complete understanding in the theory and practice of communications between the home office and the associate is a good foundation for success. Both sides may need enlightenment, not only on how to do it but also on what to say. The mechanics of communications are available just about everywhere. Consider direct dialing to Saudi Arabia and the Persian Gulf States, telex messages directly to the job site, and telephone-answering equipment for twenty-four-hour contact in home offices.

The solar system has been around for a long time, too, but explaining the "communications window" to some engineers is a considerable task. One example will suffice: It is 7 P.M. in Riyadh, Saudi Arabia, when it is 9 A.M. in Chicago. If the Chicago office starts work at 9 A.M., the Saudi partner must be contacted first thing in the morning, which means the partner must be available from 7 to 9 P.M. (normal working hours in Saudi Arabia). But remember: A Saudi does not work on Thursday and Friday and the home office is closed on Saturday and Sunday. So the communications window from Riyadh to Chicago is only open Monday to Wednesday from 9 to 11 A.M. at best, or six hours a week. A communications schedule must be worked out, and both parties may have to accommodate their personal lives to it. For example, Saturday and Sunday mornings are an excellent time to contact Middle East offices.

What the message contains is as important as the successful transmission. The partner must be drilled to send facts, and as many as can be discovered. Telex messages such as HOW WOULD YOU LIKE TO DESIGN A BRIDGE OVER THE BOSPOROUS? are worthless and agonizing, as are such mind bogglers as HAVE LEAD ON HUGE PORT PROJECT IN MIDDLE EAST. CAN'T DIVULGE NAME OF CLIENT OR

COUNTRY. PLEASE ANSWER YES OR NO BY RETURN TELEX AND, IF AFFIRMA-
TIVE, SEND PORT ENGINEER IMMEDIATELY, and so on.

In summary, the associate should be expected to contribute
the following:

- A "presence" for your firm
- A source of information about your field
- Early knowledge of specific projects
- Support for visiting staff in preparing proposals
- Knowledge of sources of financial and tax advice
- Ability to furnish or obtain local professional and support staff for your joint projects
- Knowledge of local conditions and early warning concerning emergencies that affect your operation

Formal selection of a local associate must be confirmed by
a written agreement. This document can be a private one, but
in some countries it must be registered (Egypt, Qatar, and
United Arab Emirates). The agreement should be cleared by the
associate's lawyer as well as your own, and it should serve as a
basis for future action. An agreement might include some of the
following items:

- It should be written in a tone that attributes goodwill and integrity to both parties. Resist talking down to a local associate. Give equal billing.
- Reimburse monthly if money is spent for your account.
- Don't authorize the associate to obligate you in any way, either by signing contracts, agreeing to scope or schedule changes, or by incurring debts in your name.
- The agreement should contain a carefully edited paragraph to the effect that each party will obey and respect the laws of the other country. This will take tact and patience on your part, because some western laws are offensive to other cultures. (Imagine a law called the "Corrupt Practices Act"!)
- The agreement should cover a certain period, a definite geographical area, and should describe the field of activity.
- Keep the agreement short, concise, and simple (two pages maximum). Plain language should prevail, and the agreement

should be translated into the local partner's language by your translator.

The association agreement, thus prepared, should be a good cornerstone for a successful partnership. Before you sign it, review the provisions with your new associate. Give copies to your key people, and ask that the associate's staff be informed in a like manner.

With the associate selected, the agreement signed, and a marketing plan established, now it is time for action. The associate has visited your home office, and your people have been to visit his office. If it turns out the associate has an advanced degree from a western university, speaks your language, and is a practicing professional, the future should be relatively bright. If another language is involved, now is the time to deal with the problem before the situation deteriorates. If you have an employee who speaks the language and the associate has one who speaks yours, the communication problem can be minimized. A communications plan can be worked out by your staffs, covering telephone and telex schedules, and with details about sending telexes, cables, and courier packages. A clear understanding of mail and courier reliability should be worked out, so your first joint proposal will not miss the submittal deadline. This is an unpardonable sin.

Treat your associate as you would like to be treated. Give a fair share of the credit and publicity. At the same time, resist any attempts to use you as a "ghost" consultant. In some countries, local design firms are eager to gain status, and they hide their foreign partners from clients and the general public.

Care should be exercised not to give the local associate carte blanche to deal with the joint venture's client. The local person may be "soft" when dealing with the client, because of old friendships. After all, you may be looked on as a bird of passage, and promises of future work, after the association with you is ended, are difficult for the associate to resist.

Support your associate from your home office. Count on acting as a personal purchasing agent—for maps, sunglasses, and a steering wheel for his Alfa-Romeo. Do hotel bookings, and take care of the associate's children when they visit your country.

Be patient with your associate's lack of knowledge of our laws, which you have maintained must be obeyed or you will be subjected to strong penalties. For example, if you are U.S.

based, it would be a good idea to have your lawyer and his discuss subjects like the Corrupt Practices Act, the boycott of Israel, and U.S. tax laws that affect U.S. citizens abroad. On his side, if the association is in the Middle East, the associate's lawyer might discuss the local traditions and customs which must be observed to avoid censure. If the association covers other parts of the world, such as Africa, many of these same items will apply. In Latin America, the points for complete understanding may be more subtle. Under the surface of a fast-moving commercial life, politics, traditions, and customs will present problems that must be understood by the successful foreign consultant.

Do these partnerships really work? Is it commercially attractive, professionally rewarding, and intellectually stimulating to work abroad with local professional associates? Granted the challenge is large, the failure rate is high. Complete involvement and commitment are required. If one has the professional background and experience which bring needed skills to the partnership, a foreign association in a developing market can mean success, both professional and financial.

There are outstanding cases of local associations that work on all sides, which professionals might do well to emulate. Consider ARAMCO and the other petroleum companies abroad, mining companies, and the airlines. Many of these present outstanding examples of the understanding and cooperation that work well, with local partners playing increasingly important roles. Construction contractors, too, are successful in working abroad with staffs that look like the UN Assembly. Consulting engineers can do the same, if their partners are well chosen, compatible, and if they have leadership committed to making the joint venture work.

*Nine* dos and don'ts for identifying candidates for the local-partner role follow:

1. Do enter the execution phase of the search with enthusiasm and commitment.
2. Don't give up because all the eager candidates seem to be terribly unwestern. Then your own outlook could probably stand some reorientation.
3. Do look for high-quality associates.
4. Don't expect your associate to look like an IBM executive. Remember, his grandfather may have been a nomadic tribesman.

5. Do be wary of someone who is searching for a foreign partner to act as a ghostwriter and who wants to put a name on
your design.

6. Do give thoughtful consideration to a candidate who shows
you his "back rooms," his designs and design approach,
and proudly introduces his staff.

7. Do understand that even though different ways of doing
business are common in foreign lands, basic ideas of integrity and honesty apply universally. Break off the courtship
if there's anything about the business ethics of your candidate you cannot live with.

8. Don't consider association without a simple and concise
written agreement.

9. Do commit yourself to making the venture succeed.

# CHAPTER 6

# MARKETING

Marketing—offering one's services for hire—has become a legitimate function of today's design professional. Not long ago marketing was considered degrading—downright unethical—by many consultants. One would discuss services when invited in by a client, but offering them for sale was generally limited to the publication of sterile, inarticulate business cards in the journals of the learned societies. Whenever services were offered, it was by the senior partners at a quiet luncheon meeting with a former client.

Experiences in World War II started to change the marketing process. Defense project opportunities led consulting firms to develop and expand. The war's end released such a pent-up demand for all types of nonmilitary design and construction services that it became necessary to make presentations and marketing calls on prospective clients to compete. And since the federal government required the consulting engineer to have a registered architect on the team if buildings were involved, the "architect-engineer" organization became a convenient operating form, particularly on large projects.

Architects brought good experience in making presentations since their basic training included defending designs in competitions at school. This capability began to influence even the most staid and conservative engineering firm. Visual aid material—models, renderings, and color slides—became a part of the presentation. No longer would the senior partner stand before the selection board and mumble haltingly that the firm could do a good job. Marketing had arrived.

Marketing studies, plans, and presentations occupy an important and necessary place in the operation of all design organizations. A typical midsized architectural and engineering firm will spend about 5 percent of its gross income on marketing and sales, including labor, overhead, travel, and direct costs. When this marketing budget enters the $1 million range, who needs convincing that marketing merits careful planning and controlled execution? If one reads a news release stating that a large international engineering firm has been "called in by the government of Saudi Arabia to design an airport," you can bet that competition was fierce. Probably ten or more of the world's most renowned firms were in the competition. The marketing effort had to be going on for months, and budgets of the competitors for this effort had to be big. The president of the successful firm would like you to think that it all happened because of sterling leadership and reputation. Don't you believe it—that was only a minor factor in the selection process.

In international operations, marketing is key to a successful start. One new to the field, having no overseas contracts or foreign experience record, should be forewarned: Marketing will require "venture capital," courage, and commitment. The very thought of spending the necessary time and money to do a good international marketing job typically discourages domestic managers. If a consensus of such insular minds leads to pursuing "targets of opportunity," the venture faces heavy odds; after a few years of making unsuccessful proposals on random projects, based on sparse background study and bad pricing information, the international market will usually be abandoned. But a firm really committed to foreign work will approach the task with a rational plan. Unknowns will be eliminated, strengths determined, and experienced personnel assigned to this sector.

The international marketing plan and budget need careful development by a select team. The plan should precede any formal action because it will serve as a policy instrument as well as an execution plan. Once management approves it, assigns responsibilities, and grants authority—all documented—the plan has a chance for success. Without a plan, selecting a target country, picking an associate, and setting aside an arbitrary amount of money for a one-shot marketing effort are actions which can pave the road to disaster. Yet many international ventures result from "gut feelings," and they fail for lack of a studied approach.

There is no established prototype for a marketing plan. Each organization has so many variables—size, specialties, capital, services offered, location, and staff—that universal plan format is not possible. It is more practical to define the items that should be addressed, to describe the purpose of the plan, and to establish broad policy. The amount of detail will depend on the marketing staff and the need for guidance. Then the final plan should be summarized for management so it won't have to wade through the plan's detailed instructions to field staff.

An international marketing plan will be fundamentally the same as a domestic plan. The stated purpose of each plan is to provide direction for seeking opportunities to make proposals and obtain contracts. Whatever serves well in the domestic effort will probably work abroad. Since by design this text addresses professionals already established in the domestic market, the export marketing fundamentals discussed below include only those differing from what applies to domestic marketing.

The international planning effort should produce the following:

1. A clearly defined plan for the international market to guide all company officers and employees
2. A list of "target" countries, their principal client prospects, and each country's business outlook
3. An operations plan describing positions, with target dates for full staffing
4. Goals for international marketing
5. Annual budget, including home office and foreign costs

The first step in making a marketing plan is to take inventory, doing the soul-searching self-analysis described in Chapter 1. These conclusions must be reviewed and restated in the plan. Homework and fact-finding trip completed, their results become a part of the plan. In addition, the selected associate's role should be described carefully.

It is soon time to reassess the draft marketing plan and restudy the preliminary budget established at the end of Chapter 3. It might not be astute to revise this budget drastically. After all, it was approved by the board of directors following considerable discussion. But if the first budget now appears to be unrealistic, it needs to be reworked to retain management's commitment for foreign work.

A very logical and common attitude that may be evident in your organization is the temptation to wait for the local associate to produce a request for proposal. While not denying the possibility of such a miracle, I would advise you to proceed with the marketing plan and to include the foreign associate in it as a full member of the team.

The marketing plan will call for placing an experienced marketer in the foreign associate's office or in an independent location nearby. The marketer must be identified, briefed, and made a party to the marketing plan to become your effective "man on the scene," the third ingredient of the foreign venture, in addition to your firm's commitment and the foreign associate. Assuming your services are good, these three ingredients should produce requests for proposal.

The first person assigned permanently to the foreign post should know the firm and the services to be marketed. The ideal nominee is becoming more difficult to find, reflecting the increase in number of two-career families and declining interest in foreign assignments among midcareer personnel. The best solution can be to employ an experienced international marketer to work temporarily with an experienced company professional who would not accept a permanent overseas assignment. After six months of foreign service the experienced newcomer should have a good background, and the veteran employee can be reassigned to the home office.

The report of the fact-finding mission (Chapter 3) will be a governing factor in shaping the final marketing plan. A careful analysis of apparent opportunities should be made, with close scrutiny accorded the most promising prospective clients. Projects known to be in the annual budgets of these organizations should be checked against the firm's strengths, then priorities assigned. The more thorough this research, the more effective the marketer will be after arriving on the scene. Until the marketer is settled abroad and learns what sort of help to expect from the local associate, the marketing strategy can hardly be planned.

Are company brochures, project data sheets, slide presentations, and other marketing tools suitable for the marketer's new assignment? If not, priority needs to be given to preparing new material, because of the typical long lead time consultants require to produce and approve brochures.

The marketing plan and budget can be completed with few unknowns. Once the target country and the associate are selected, the business goal must be set by a reverse calculation. What volume of business must be generated to pay for the marketing expenses? A realistic estimate can be made by first reviewing the average size of contracts being awarded in your field. Assuming that no plans to double or triple the gross volume of your business are envisaged, it is prudent to set goals requiring steady growth. Annual growth in billings of 20 to 30 percent maintained over a three-year period might be realistic, for example. At this time a helpful exercise is to run out several examples of the plan, including a "worst case" scenario, with a contingency for "bailout." The existence of this contingency plan does not have to be publicized at a mass meeting, but it may be very convenient for later discussions.

Having established a goal—expected dollar volume of contracts—some exercise should be conducted related to the probability of obtaining that amount of business. Estimate the "hit" ratio: How many proposals on the average must be made to be awarded a contract? If the ratio normally achieved by your firm is 10 to 1, proposals must be submitted for 10 times the goal. The ratio is higher for many foreign public works contracts because a number of qualifications must be submitted just to get short-listed—that is, named as one of the prequalified firms from which the owner would like to receive a proposal. So it might be necessary to identify twenty opportunities for each contract won. We all have our own ways of rationalizing sales efforts versus awards, but it is clear that it may be a year before the first contract is signed. The marketing effort must be big enough and long enough to provide a fair trial.

Marketing opportunities can be expanded by several obvious methods. If a particularly attractive client has a project planned requiring a major amount of services that your firm alone cannot provide, consider a joint venture with an organization with outstanding capability but insufficient staff or foreign experience.

In developing countries inexperienced in dealing with design firms, selection often depends on mutual trust and confidence developed between individuals. This established trust may be a greater factor than technical background when the time comes to select a consultant for a new project.

One successful approach in the selection process is to discuss the project with the person who has the authority to make selection and to lay most, if not all, of your cards on the table. Suggest that you will associate with another competent firm which will perform the part of the design that your expertise does not cover. Propose that you will personally be responsible for the quality and on-time delivery of the professional work. This approach may get your firm on the short list. It has succeeded with foreign governments and U.S. agencies. You must be very sure of your position with the client and also be confident that the new associate will deliver the promised items on time and of high quality.

Another way to widen opportunities with an old client, with whom your firm has a good track record, is to seek subcontracts from other consultants or contractors. For example, in the petroleum and petrochemical industries, the engineer-constructors look on any non-process-related construction as a minor irritant. They are prone to submit "courtesy" quotations on housing, office buildings, schools, clinics, and other support facilities included in a project. They have no real desire or capability for designing such features. Seek out this type of subcontract, for it will be simple to manage, since you will be working for professionals, and could result very profitably because your production costs may be significantly below those of the engineer-constructor.

Now, back to the budget. Using the guidelines discussed above, make rational assumptions to reach conclusions about the target country. Then schedule marketing effort at a steady rate—even if you stumble into a big contract in the first month, marketing should continue at the planned rate. Otherwise, there may be a long, dry spell before your next contract. Don't let the marketing effort abate after the first contract award. In spite of popular concepts, there is no record of any architectural and engineering firm ever being awarded more work than it could complete.

The marketing plan will be an operations plan for your man on the scene. It should contain the following:

1. Goals
2. Implementation
3. Support
4. Marketing criteria
5. Desirable project types
6. Reporting instructions
7. Proposals
8. Annexes
   a. Copy of fact-finding report
   b. Power of attorney
   c. Standard forms
   d. Sources of professional assistance
9. Budget

### TYPICAL ANNUAL BUDGET FOR FOREIGN BASED MARKETER

*Assumptions*
1. Employee and wife, stationed in Riyadh, Saudi Arabia for 2-year contract
2. Transportation from U.S. East Coast
3. No household goods shipped
4. 1984 rates and prices

*Mobilization*
1. Salary                                      $ 70,000
2. Payroll OH (taxes, insurance, etc.)           21,000
3. Air transportation (2) (economy class)         4,200
4. Air freight (personal effects)                 2,000
5. Store household goods                          2,500
6. Temporary living costs U.S. and Saudi
   Arabia—30 days                                 6,000
7. Rent                                          30,000

| 8. Furniture | 10,000 |
|---|---|
| 9. Misc. and contingencies @ 15% | 14,600 |

| Subtotal | $160,300 |

**Operations**

| 1. Office space | $ 12,000 |
|---|---|
| 2. Travel budget | 5,000 |
| 3. Entertainment | 5,000 |
| 4. Phone/Telex | 5,000 |
| 5. Secretary | 12,000 |
| 6. Driver | 8,000 |
| 7. Car expense | 2,400 |
| 8. Proposal costs | 5,000 |
| 9. Car (2-year life) | 8,000 |
| 10. Home office support | 30,000 |
| 11. Contingencies @ 10% | 9,240 |
| Subtotal | $101,640 |
| Total | $261,940 |

The marketing plan must be developed with discretion. No two international design firms would have similar plans. In fact many organizations have no formal guidelines, according to many of my colleagues in other firms. Ideas of what a marketing plan should look like range from "no plan at all," or ad hoc procedures and plans on the back of a small envelope all the way up to a 4-inch-thick ring binder with maps, calendars, and everything except a pocket for headache pills. Martin French, a well-known British consultant, has said that his checklist for planning a visit to a new market area is seventeen pages long. So your marketing plans can be painted on any size canvas but should reflect study of the firm's specialties, peculiarities of the organization, and market conditions.

The great need to provide clarity and direction is fully appreciated when one remembers that the purpose of the plan is to guide an often lonely and frustrated associate toward the goal of getting contracts in a seemingly hostile environment. Will the plan make sense to this person in the wee hours of the morning when the power has failed in Mogadisho, Somalia?

Designers are often accused of believing that their designs are an end in themselves and of forgetting that their drawings are merely a form of communication with craftsmen and other professions. Planners are enthusiastic about plans and frequently produce reams of documents for one small program. Resist the urge to build monuments to planning. In the first place, your marketing plan for entering the new area describes a method for learning about opportunities for your firm. If you knew all about this subject, you would go to the country, meet the client, make a proposal, and sign the contract. Nothing to it—no plan required. But when the prospect has to be found and developed, a systematic approach is most productive and that requires a document prepared to keep the troops headed toward the goal.

Most planners handle the jargon of the profession and the network analysis with the greatest of ease. There is a tendency for them to encounter "soft ground" when coping with details of foreign operations. Imagine trying to develop a critical path for construction of a brick building without knowing anything about the bricklayer's trade? Someone familiar with local conditions must advise the market planners. The fact-finding trip (Chapter 3) developed a list of local customs, events, and conditions that would affect the marketing process. Study these reports carefully and question the fact finders before finalizing the plan. Get all of the "bad news" into the plan at this stage.

The acid test of the marketing plan will come during the first year. It should be realized that all the goals established in the comfort of the home office will not be attainable. Midcourse corrections will be necessary, and the assigned staff should be conditioned to this fact. Persistence is a virtue, but there may come times when losses must be cut, and new strategies adopted.

### Typical Situations Requiring Changed Plans

- All the important ministry offices and some of the best marketing targets are in Riyadh, the capital of Saudi Arabia. Being from the Eastern Province, our associate's best clients and contacts are in Dammam. Our plan called for our marketer to be located in Riyadh. If we locate him there, our associate would be three hundred miles away.

  - SOLUTION.  Locate the marketer in the associate's Dammam office for the first six months. When these two people have proved that they can work together, take another look at the main Saudi Arabian office. A base will probably always be needed in the capital city, but perhaps our man should have his main office in Dammam.

- After our man arrived in Panama, it was discovered that our associate was not on the greatest of terms with the public works minister. The two were contemporaries and bitter political rivals. In Panama, the cabinet ministers advise the government and the president on all problems in the same manner as a small corporation might operate.

   - SOLUTION.   Discount the public works department as a target for prime contracts. Be alert for joint ventures and subcontracts with acceptable firms. Devote attention to power projects and anything *not* in the public works area. Look to the private sector. Test Colombia and Costa Rica for prospects. Keep an eye on public works and be alert for a change in ministers.

- On arrival in Lagos, our man learns of a request for proposals for design of several universities. The local associate has no real capabilities. The architect-engineer selection is by a committee whose adviser is an expatriate architect who "wrote the book" on tropical school design.

   - SOLUTION.   Hold off on implementing the marketing plan. Assist the local associate in putting together a team of engineers to share in the proposal and to satisfy the "Nigerianization" requirement. Send for proposal support from the home office, headed by a senior partner who wrote a highly respected text about space planning in colleges. After the contract is negotiated, start the marketing plan.

The first steps have now been taken:

1. The decision to export was made (Chapter 1).
2. Skills were inventoried and strengths identified (Chapter 2).
3. The fact-finding trip was completed (Chapter 3).
4. Our associate was selected (Chapter 5).
5. The marketing plan has been developed (Chapter 6).

The next step is to put the plan in operation without haste and to make revisions when required. A successful marketing operation requires information from the field on investment programs and projects. The market study phase (Chapter 2) outlined methods for organizing an intelligence-gathering system. The search for prospects should be continuous, and a data base should be maintained for each target country. A major task for the foreign-based marketer will be to maintain a flow of up-to-date information about the projects being tracked. The man on the scene should develop sources, check the information collected, and telex the news to the home office in its standard format. The home office should also collect information from its sources, for frequently news about foreign projects originates with banks or insurance circles.

Rumor and scandals make great cocktail hour conversations but do nothing for home office morale or the achievement of marketing goals. Stories of failures by others, for example, have little place in the reporting system. A good marketer will develop a positive outlook and will report facts. It is true that top management usually wants to know what the competition is doing and what they bid on priced proposals. In countries where proposals are opened in public, a great effort should be made to obtain the correct names and bid prices of the competition.

Preparation of proposals on large projects is very costly, as will be discussed in Chapter 11, and will consume large portions of the marketing budget in one gulp. If your consulting firm's proposals to one particular client are consistently high, it may be necessary to refrain from making further proposals to it or to reorient your proposal philosophy. This situation has occurred in rapidly developing countries, particularly with certain agencies. The huge Yanbu and Jubail projects in Saudi Arabia are good examples of programs where wide discrepancies in bidding have cost unsuccessful foreign consultants great sums of money. A project with a $10 million design fee may require a $100,000 outlay just for the proposal effort. Several unsuccessful proposals in this price range will upset the most committed board of directors. The marketer's job is to determine pricing levels for consulting work before submitting firm proposals. If a solid professional design effort cannot be furnished for the going prices, it would be discreet and pragmatic to withdraw from that sector of the market. A complete "lessons learned" review should be made of the failed proposal, and if no discrepancies are found, the decision to withdraw may avoid a costly loss.

The foreign-based marketer, whose role will be discussed in more detail in several later chapters, must sharpen personal awareness. Sources of information should be continually broadened—and nurtured—to ensure that a true perspective of the market is obtained. Lacking an attitude of awareness and an understanding of cultural differences, the international marketer will be severely handicapped. For this reason, good international marketing people are obviously not easy to find and are difficult to develop.

There is a dichotomy in describing marketing in a rational, numbers-oriented way while advising flexibility, insight, and the avoidance of excess planning. Certainly, success in dealing with other cultures, which often are not as numbers-oriented as those of industrialized countries, will require degrees of patience and compromise not usually found in professionals who operate in the domestic market. The foreign marketer often must build a bridge between company management, so rigidly rational and analytical, and the client whose culture and environment make it less rigid, rather indefinite, and flexible. Such bridge building will be discussed throughout the text.

This chapter described the international market more in principle than in detail, with emphasis on planning and flexibility. Marketing plans were outlined and an example of a budget for a target country was provided. The following list of dos and don'ts summarizes the main points:

- Do plan international marketing efforts with care, imagination, and flexibility.
- Don't rely on "gut feelings."
- Do eliminate unknowns.
- Don't expect to westernize the international market.
- Do revise, reassess, and restructure plans and budgets to fit changing market conditions.
- Don't minimize the importance of selecting a qualified marketer for the foreign post.
- Do set attainable goals.
- Don't overestimate the "hit" ratio.
- Don't slow marketing efforts because new contracts are awarded.
- Do resist building monuments to planners.

- Don't overlook the need for prompt reporting and frank evaluation of prospects.
- Do learn about the competition.
- Don't pursue clients who have established a pattern of pricing which will not support quality design.
- Do remain fast on your feet—flexible in a rational way. Know when to cut your losses.

# CHAPTER 7

# GETTING ALONG IN OTHER CULTURES

The importance of cross-cultural relations should be well understood before one undertakes the management of a foreign operation. The risk analysis commonly includes economic and political risk. For venturers in the export market, culture risk may be the least known but the most hazardous. Insurance is available for economic and political risk, but how can one hedge against failure to cope with cultural differences detected too late—usually after a contract is lost, a manager resigns, or bank balances are depleted?

What do we mean by culture? There are many meanings, but the one that applies to our industry is "training of the mind, manners, and tastes or the results of such training." It is said that culture accounts for everything about the other person that we do not understand: why Muhammadans practice polygamy, why the British drive on the left, or why the Spanish dine late. At home we have no lack of cultural differences. Coastal people are noisy and outgoing, mountain folk conservative and quiet. Southerners eat grits, Northerners oatmeal. Saint Louis people drink beer. Perceptions of cultural difference are endless. However, the knowledge that there are domestic differences in culture does not prepare us for managing business in the export world.

When you first arrive in a foreign country, the culture shock hits hard. Some of the shock is physiological—it's hotter or colder than you expected, you are tired and somewhat desynchronized from jet lag. The biggest effect may be psychological—the babel of new accents and languages, the strange odors and unfamiliar dress. The taxi may have no meter, the hotel room is cold, and the hot water faucet has the letter *C* on it. All this is the beginning of culture shock, and you have only just arrived. Just wait until you get to the office!

The things that are bewildering in the first days are not the real differences that will sink the joint venture or make the dam leak. What was observed on the way from the plane to the hotel are surface differences, which are unimportant by themselves, but serve to indicate that things will soon be different. Be aware that in the new market area there will be some obvious, and some not so obvious, new factors affecting your daily, social, and family life. Now is a good time to restudy the material on local culture that was gathered in the homework phase.

The first priority is to work out a personal plan for surviving in the new culture. Any foreign post, whether your last assignment was Managua, Manila, or Milwaukee will provide some culture shock. There are many examples, but some which I recall most vividly follow.

- *The Backward Ripsaw.* Arriving at Cristobal (by the Panama Canal) on a ship from New York, we went directly through the locks to Balboa. The canal transit gave me a good opportunity to study the people working in the locks areas. The big surprise came from watching a carpenter rip a 1-inch board with a handsaw, holding the saw with the teeth on the top side, and cutting away from himself. In spite of having the saw "upside down" by my standards, the carpenter was ripping the board, in the oppressive tropical heat, at a very fast rate. My thoughts were—"Is this a clue to understanding Panama? Do they do everything backward?"

- *Time Concepts.* An attitude that affects both business and home life is the concept of time. Most cultures are not as schedule-oriented as we are in the west. A saying exists in Spanish and Arabic—"Tomorrow, God willing." In Libya, when wanting to indicate a short time, a local person says, "in five minutes"—which can last four or five hours. A longer space of time would be described as—"after tomorrow"—which could include from next week to forever. In Europe, Latin America, and the Middle East punctuality is not a religion. The well-mannered executive (which includes practically all) will have you ushered into a waiting room, served tea or coffee, and left sitting in solitary splendor for an appropriate length of time. Just when you have begun to think you have been forgotten (maybe a half hour), your host will appear and explain how happy he is to see you, in spite of his hectic schedule. After pondering the reasoning for this charade for years, I can only classify it as charming cultural courtesy based on a different concept of time.

- **Meetings.** First meetings with important people in the Middle East tend to be "getting to know you" sessions. The meeting is called a *majlis*, and there may be other people present whose purpose is unrelated to yours. The ever polite and formal host chats with each visitor, in no particular order, while the guests consume large numbers of small cups of mint tea or Turkish coffee. The other guests enjoy your unfamiliarity with the customs and may give opinions about your mission in their country. I was in a session with the city manager of Doha, Qatar, when the guests included a butcher who wanted permission to kill an animal, another man who was a bedouin friend of the family, an irate citizen who did not want to have his front porch cut off in a street-widening project, and two of my British competitors. The latter were amazed at my shocking ignorance of local customs. This concept of time affords the local official a chance to form an impression of a business visitor before entering into serious discussion.

Cultural differences are disturbing, but when taken one at a time, most newcomers can cope very well—especially if they include in their new environment some familiar and pleasant diversions to ease the situation. In many posts, foreigners will have to provide their own recreation, such as audio and video tapes, reading material, home study courses, and hobbies. If other foreigners are around, social and sports groups will develop. Becoming a recluse will not be very helpful in the long term, and, frequently, odd behavior may surface. Telltale signs are unkempt appearance, dirty clothing, lack of sleep, vacant stares, mumbling, and lack of eye contact. We have all heard of people on remote assignment who became "island happy," which is just another condition resulting from exposure to new culture and hostile environment.

The mere fact that the diet available at the new post is not the same as at home is very unnerving to some people. Visitors from the main office are overwhelmed with endless complaints about the available food. Very often newcomers have weight gains from changed diets. Foreign duty thus has its drawbacks, and the success or failure of a new operation may depend on the ability of senior professionals to cope with cultural changes that affect home life.

The best-adjusted international employee is usually one who tries to understand the new culture and who respects local customs and traditions. It is not necessary to take on local coloration. In fact, as a professional, one is expected to retain some national traits. After all, the client wants transfer of technology from enlightened visitors.

I remember a manager who had lived in France so long that he had adopted the complete lifestyle, accent, and mannerisms of the country. An important client called one day and complained of his treatment at the hands of this person. "Don't send me any more pseudo-Frenchmen. We hired a U.S. firm to do this important job," he said. Perhaps not a fair perception—but the client wanted another image, and clients aren't always fair.

The business implications of a new culture are even more important to success in an export market. The expatriate employees will soon adjust to new customs and ways of life. If they can't make the transition, resignations and replacements will result so the condition is almost self-correcting.

With experience a successful exporter will have mastered the art of selecting good candidates for foreign assignment. In fact, help is available from industrial psychologists who have devised tests which can be used to determine suitability for overseas environments. An applicant is given a group of multiple-choice questions, and the answers are entered in a calculator programmed to grade the test. This tool may reduce the assignment of misfits.

Although it was stated earlier that what worked well domestically would probably be useful in marketing internationally, this premise may be incorrect when applied to an individual's ability to adapt to local conditions. A few examples may help illustrate how daily operations are affected:

- Early in my career I spent several years as a survey party chief. At home the party chief was responsible for the survey instrument and carried it on the job. The byword at TVA was "That instrument is expensive. If there is an accident, you must be beaten up as badly as it is." In other words, guard the instrument with your life. Things were different at the Panama Canal. After a week of running hydrographic survey baselines along the bank of the canal, I noticed that every time I set up the instrument, there would be a big young man standing two or three paces behind me, observing my every move. Finally I got curious and asked him, "What part do you play in this operation?" He replied, "I carry that instrument you have been toting around all week. Every time I am supposed to pick it up, you put it on your shoulder and run off." Thus I learned that I had been "losing face" by my lack of recognition of local customs. I handed over the heavy transit, and he was once again proud to be doing his assigned task. Production improved notably.

- Financial affairs are controlled at the very top in family operated or tribal firms. There are no discussions of cash management at board meetings or in front of joint-venture partners. In fact, the shaikh gives explicit instructions on disbursement of cash to his accountant in closed-door meetings. Imagine the shock when the American partner's leader pointed an extended index finger at the chest of the older brother (the Saudi Arabian partner's chairman) and said in a loud voice, "We demand that you transfer our payments by telex to the United States within twenty-four hours after the client has paid you!" This approach is not a recommended way to make a point in the Middle East. Prolonged private discussions are required to handle such matters—and lots of face-saving tactics must be used to get movement on such questions.

- In some countries, decisions cannot be made without clearance from a higher power. For example, in Italy, which has a matriarchal culture, the mother sometimes has the last word. Considerable time and money was devoted to selecting a resident engineer, an Italian, for a large construction project in Africa. Everything appeared to be in order, including the client's approval. When the candidate, a forty-year-old bachelor, came to my office to pick up his plane tickets and last-minute instructions, he regretfully announced that his mother would not give permission for him to leave Italy!

European cultures have been discussed, investigated, and understood for a long time. Indeed, with the development of multinational corporations and international banks, a way of business has been developed which takes account of cultural needs. Books have been written, such as *The Americanization of Europe*, by Edward A. McCreary, and *Main Street Italy*, by Irving R. Levine, which will accelerate one's understanding of the effect of European culture on doing business your normal way. The problems presented by these well-studied cultures are difficult but not impossible. After all, every small town in the United States has an Italian restaurant; French wine is available everywhere, as are Swiss watches and Belgian lace.

The real cultural dilemmas are met when one gets into the rapidly developing countries of Africa, Asia, and the Middle East. The cultural change forced on the people of Saudi Arabia by the discovery of oil and the global energy crisis is unequaled in history. In ten years or less, what existed there has been transformed so that the country is almost unrecognizable to those who visited it in the 1960s. The Saudi culture has been battered by all the world, and the kingdom's citizens have adapted to the abrupt change in a remarkable manner. But in many ways, Saudi Arabia is more conservative and socially rigid now than it was before the oil boom. Rapid progress in the material sense has resulted in a sort of cultural backlash, and old traditions have been strengthened. Controls affecting foreigners have been increased. There is a tendency for Saudi families to mix less with foreigners than in the recent past. In fact, careful attention to cultural differences is becoming more important than ever for the expatriate in Saudi Arabia and other conservative Moslem countries.

Although the change has been most dramatic in Saudi Arabia because of its wealth of natural resources, its historical and religious importance, and its strategic location, there have been gigantic shocks in other Middle East countries. Consider Libya, said to have had the lowest per capita income of any country when it gained independence in 1951. Until the production of oil in 1961, Libya's economy was hardly developed. But soaring petroleum export earnings financed huge investments: a national airline, a highway system, public housing, universal education, and a flood of unheard-of amenities. Change came so rapidly that an overthrow by a religious archconservative regime has been in effect for more than a decade.

Iran, whose culture almost defies perception by westerners,

is another example of a market that has taken its toll on exporters. The government of Iran attempted to transform the country into an industrial nation with a twenty-year program. The result, in simplistic terms, was that the methods used and the culture shock were so harsh that the change could be neither accomplished nor absorbed.

Saudi Arabia, Libya, and Iran are well-known examples of important export markets where the successful operations of design professionals have been affected more by cultural factors than by inept financial management or poor professional performance.

Therein lies the challenge to present positive guidance for dealing with cultural changes in a way that will help achieve the marketing and operational goals. Historical examples should be used to illustrate situations brought on by failure to recognize cultural background. Where possible, solutions will be suggested for eliminating conflict, so the premise that foreign markets offer good opportunities for well-planned operations will prevail.

It is important to properly identify the source of roadblocks that confront operations abroad. The problems one has in a domestic market do not melt away when you enter the international field. Cultural inequality cannot be blamed for all failures any more than the weather can be used to excuse shoddy thinking or bad design. The world cannot be understood by labeling people broadly. All Latins are not brown-eyed, dark-haired, and mañana-oriented. There are bad French restaurants; not all Italians eat pasta daily. Develop awareness and persistence in identifying the root causes for trouble. Was it something about the culture? Did we understand each other? Were we both talking about the same subject?

We planned a fact-finding trip without much regard to the cultural differences. It was assumed at the time that the information sought could be obtained by a capable team with minimal coaching on how to get along in another culture. After all, the team would be dealing with top people who would be bilingual or multilingual and who could speak the team's language. The exploratory mission could be successful without the emphasis that would be placed on culture when supervising technical employees or dealing with design problems. That fact-finding trip, as you might expect, tripped some alarms. Some of the local technocrats wondered whether they wanted our company in their country and whether they could deal with us in a business situation. On another occasion when I was with some friends at the Panamanian Society of Engineers and Architects, one of them said, "We had a visit today from a prominent U.S. engineer who wants to associate with us. This guy may be O.K. but he was dressed in full technicolor." I decided to defend my countryman and urged my friends not to be so critical. Their reply was—in almost one voice—"But you are one of us—your dress and appearance is just like ours!" It is not necessary to pretend that you are something you are not—but particularly in countries where there is a national costume, like Saudi Arabia, it is thoughtful to adopt a conservative style that reflects what you might wear when calling on a person of similar status in your own country.

Frequently, it is difficult to realize what is going on behind the scenes during negotiations. It may be well to stop and review with your group after a day's negotiations with prospective clients or associates. For example, a group of architects and engineers went to Chile to negotiate a joint-venture agreement with a local firm, involving the design of a large commercial building. The actions of the local group completely confused the "gringos," who, after finally negotiating an acceptable contract, reported that during the first three days nothing tangible was accomplished. There had been just one long meeting each afternoon, with no agendas, no decisions, but many trivial and endless discussions. Then on the fourth day there was no meeting—just a long, vinous lunch at a posh country club, lasting until five-thirty. On the fifth day, the meeting began promptly at 10 A.M. with an agenda. By lunch the joint-venture agreement, in principle, was initialed by all and turned over to the lawyers for final drafting. The visitors left for home the next day.

The Americans were nonplussed. All that precious time wasted when they could have accomplished the same thing in three days. Some time later I discussed the situation with a Chilean friend who knew the local firm well. "What your American friends did not realize is that we do not rely on bank references, brochures, balance sheets, or recommendations. We don't even have any D&B credit reports. If they existed, we would not believe them." The negotiation actually began on the day the visitors arrived in Santiago, but they did not realize it. The reason that there was no meeting on the fourth day was that the local firm's partners had met that morning and finally decided to go with the Americans in the joint venture, in spite of the "hard sell" of the Yankee team leader. The visitors were judged to be very competent, although very naive about taxation and profits (too low). The technical leader was thought to be an able professional and, furthermore, to have some emotions—a man with whom they could relate. The big lunch was a Latin way of showing acceptance, although not much was said about it. My Latin friend said, "These fellows did not realize they had been examined and negotiated with for three days!" Not an unusual experience. Learning from other cultures takes a while. That is why your awareness of such differences should start before you leave home.

If you wonder what motivates your potential client, consider background. Try to measure any reactions against the cultural background. When you realize that the planning minister, who has a Ph.D. from Harvard, is the son of a bedouin who is still following his livestock in the desert, you will begin to understand. It may be that your system of values is not the same as that of the person on the other side of the table. Why shouldn't someone else have a different concept of time?

It is easy to get a false sense of understanding about the way another person thinks because of outward appearances. If your associate's education is parallel to your own, it doesn't mean the person has the same values. There was a senior engineer in our Panama office who had worked with me in Florida, and we were good social friends. He was a fine professional, and I relied heavily on his knowledge of Panama. On a field trip to the interior, he introduced me to his father. I was surprised to meet a *campesino*—a barefoot peasant farmer, who preferred to squat on his heels rather than to sit in a chair. I was impressed by the elder man's dignity and pride. Yet the difference in the cultural and environmental background of these two men was incredible. How could I expect my friend to have the same values that I and my partners had?

It is not possible—nor is it necessary—to understand exactly what another person thinks or how that person will react. However, one is better prepared to cope with important problems if possessed of a latent awareness that an adversary may frequently be marching to the beat of a different drummer.

A direct, rational approach to engineering design and construction problems is not always helpful in other cultures. This shocking lesson was learned early in foreign service. A large supermarket building in Panama collapsed during construction. Fortunately, no one was on the site, and there were no casualties. Each interested party—owner, contractor, engineer, and architect—hired expert witnesses to affix the blame for the failure. Our firm was one of the experts, and we went about the task in textbook fashion. Photographs, tests, depositions, new designs, and formal reports were produced. There was no doubt about our findings.

On the other hand, one of the other experts was a famous Mexican consultant. He flew into town one evening and gave a lecture on a nonrelated subject to the local engineering society. The next day he lunched with this group, after which, accompanied by a large party, he toured the site for less than an hour. Then he returned to Mexico and in due course his report was received. In a one-page letter, the first two paragraphs gave thanks for hospitality and praise for the status of the profession in Panama. The next paragraph described the failed structure, with lavish praise for the outstanding design and construction. The last paragraph acknowledged the unfortunate disaster, and the writer detailed certain changes he recommended if the building were to be rebuilt. Incidentally, these were precisely the same changes which were recommended in our report. His efforts were received with wide acclaim, while ours were never heard from again.

I am sure the Mexican engineer (a really brilliant professional) obtained more work in Panama as a result of his short visit. Our approach was too dogmatic and perhaps somewhat arrogant for the local culture. The solution offered by the Mexican consultant de-emphasized the accident. The building was completed, and I believe that the costs were shared by all parties. This lesson in statesmanship, not to mention gamesmanship, has tempered my reactions to problems faced in other cultures.

The locus of power in foreign organizations is often not obvious to outsiders. When there is a doubt, culture may play a role. In the Middle East the *shaikh*, the tribal leader, is the chief executive officer. The younger brother may have a Ph.D. from Stanford Business School and an impeccable western facade. He will negotiate very positively and make decisions right and left. But after protracted meetings it may be noticed that some of the earlier decisions have been reversed or amended without any explanation. This is an unfailing sign that the "power" has reviewed the work of the younger brother and made arbitrary changes. The agreements you thought had been made with a delegated authority fell apart! This is a very discouraging development, because you have played all of your best cards and used up your negotiating currency. The result may be that your joint venture has a terminal illness.

There is no simple formula for recovering from failing to recognize power. The obvious relief is to investigate power structures carefully and to involve the leader in the discussions. This might possibly reduce arbitrary changes but is not a guarantee that a major stockholder, a prince, or a mother is not lurking in the wings with power to edit the fine print of your contract. The situation is most prevalent in family businesses—in Africa, the Middle East, southern Europe, and even Texas. Be aware, and detect this condition in an early stage. In doing so, much time, money, and patience may be saved.

In a similar vein, foreign visitors are frequently allowed to bargain with the "picadors" in early meetings. Saudi Arabian tales include that of the busy shaikh who, unable to be in two places at once, sent his chauffeur to deal with a visiting delegation for a few days. The visitors thought negotiations had begun! But after much delay and haggling with the picador, the real power took over and bargained with the weakened foe on entirely different points.

If you have identified the power unequivocally, firmly but graciously refuse to take part in the early skirmishes without that person's presence. Let your picadors handle his picadors.

Cultural differences are an important factor in foreign operations. Often it is impossible to differentiate between personality traits and cultural motivation. It is challenging and rewarding to study the new scene for values which are different and to learn which ones are important. After some time one becomes at home with a part of the culture. But it may be that much of the culture, particularly in Asia and the Far East, will be elusive. It is, I believe, important to make an ally of time. Make it work for you in achieving your goals. Listen, observe, digest, file, and test before reaching any firm conclusion about what motivates your foreign clients and associates. And above all, every person assigned to foreign operations should be given some preparation in understanding the new culture.

Finally, it is demeaning to your foreign associates and clients, as well as your own organization, to think that cross-cultural understanding can be achieved in a short period. I met the president of a large American engineering organization on his first visit to Beirut, Lebanon. His greeting was, "We have fifteen minutes before we meet the client. Bring me up to speed on the Middle East before we get to his office!" This man and his organization did not succeed in the Middle East market. He never did understand the reasons for his failure, which had much to do with lack of respect for cultural differences. As the saying goes, "He never knew what hit him!"

# CHAPTER 8

# YOUR MAN
# ON THE SCENE

When consultants begin to export services, usually the "traveling partner" gets the marketing assignment. The selection process is simple. The unique qualifications for the job are willingness to endure extensive foreign travel and patience to deal with demanding clients.

Some of the leading firms in the consulting profession still get along with a loosely structured network of associates and agents that has grown erratically over the years. Their traveling partner may visit once or twice a year to deliver a new supply of brochures, take everyone to lunch, and to exhort the agent to increase activities on the consultant's behalf. This was an adequate system in its day, which ended in the early seventies. Increased size of foreign projects, intense competition, and the need for local association have made it necessary to use better procedures.

Semiannual visits by the traveling partner are no longer adequate means of keeping in touch with opportunities and maintaining relationships with associates or managing resident project directors. Indeed, when there is an ongoing project, the client will want someone with authority on hand who can discuss contractual matters as well as make commitments on performance and delivery. There's also the possibility of the discussion of new contracts for additional work. More often, though, the client feels a need to chat with a partner, a vice president, or someone considered a counterpart in ranking on the organization chart. The most efficient system for finding new contracts abroad is not through the international traveler but by stationing a permanent employee in a selected market area. Equipped with credentials and status, your "man on the scene" will become part of the local business community.

Except for a small number of very strong firms, international consultants have rarely stationed lone executives abroad. As a result, there is no long tradition, particularly for American firms, regarding selection of international representatives. Nevertheless, firms that have overlooked the development of executives for overseas assignments now find it necessary to do so to protect their share of the market and to handle operational problems. On the other hand, consulting firms from other countries—Japan, Germany, and the United Kingdom—have long recognized the necessity of a permanent presence in developing market areas. Their employees eagerly accept foreign asssignment as a way of career advancement, without much concern for the hardship aspects of the new post. It is normal to find vice presidents of these firms in such places as Dammam, Panama, Bangkok, or Lagos where American firms have few representatives.

What should your man on the scene be doing? How can the person function best when representing your firm in the local market? First and foremost, your representative should not be a one-person band involved in design or management contracts. If tied down with demanding operational duties, he will not be able to develop leads, make proposals, or negotiate contracts. Not only that, your person must develop status and maintain it. To deal successfully with the client's top people, he must not be categorized as "one of the blokes in the design office." This matter of *face* should be observed to protect his negotiating stance, since the client does not want to do business with an underling.

A potential candidate should have the following major attributes:

■ *Professional Competence.* To be on an equal level with the client and the client's staff, your person should have a university degree in his specialty and should radiate professional competence. Your representative should be able to discuss the technical aspects of the client's project, as well as current developments in his area of expertise. Furthermore, the person should be able to "step up to the blackboard," to analyze a design and criticize it when appropriate. It's a must to have the ability to put together a project description, after thoroughly debriefing the client's staff, and to delineate a scope of work under less than ideal conditions. I remember one such company representative in Libya, a talented architect, who would wind up discussions of a new project with some rapidly drawn sketches, replete with palm trees, fountains, and the much desired green shrubs and grass in full growth. The prospective client could hardly wait to move in!

- *Maturity.* Your man must be physically tough enough to stand the rigors of environment and travel in addition to being flexible enough—mentally and emotionally—to adapt to new cultures. Above all, the person must have mature powers of observation and judgment. During the early days, his reports will be vital to maintaining management commitment. It may cool support for the marketing program if he overemphasizes discomfort and impatience with short-term inconvenience, rather than confidence in success. Your resident representative must have the endurance to do a good job despite apparent hardships.

- *Adaptability.* Your representative should generally relate to new people, languages, customs, and traditions. Without being as gregarious and superficially friendly as the public relations officer for a brewer, your person should be able to understand and tolerate, yet not take on, local color. Relations with local bureaucrats and the client's staff must enhance your image and maintain credibility.

The best place to find a person with professional competence, maturity, and adaptability may be your own staff. A home-grown representative who understands the firm—its strengths, weaknesses, and policies—is precisely what this sensitive overseas position requires. If candidates with international inclinations can be identified at home, this by itself is almost reason enough to enter the market.

But don't lessen the qualifications too much to accommodate a weak nominee. It would be far better to recruit a capable internationalist from outside than to take a chance with a misfit. A bad selection for an important international assignment can cost great sums of money and ruin fragile commitment to an export program.

A possible alternative solution to foreign representation is to cover marketing needs in specific foreign areas from the home office. This system, which uses two people who alternate for short periods, has many defects. The foreign client wants to feel a personal relationship with your man on the scene. Business develops slowly and at an uneven pace. If your company representative is constantly changing, perhaps during prolonged negotiations, the stage is set for failure. It is impossible for alternating traveling representatives to build the necessary rapport that the firm must establish with potential clients abroad.

During the early days of overseas assignment your agent might go abroad in "bachelor" status, then bring the family as soon as suitable arrangements could be made. But the single's life in many developing countries is not very rewarding. Unless there is sufficient out-of-country leave or business travel to provide relief from weather and hostile environment, the unmarried executive tends to become unproductive.

Another arrangement could be to station your man in a centrally located city with suitable resources for the family: Panama, Singapore, Abidjan (Ivory Coast), or Bahrain, for example. This may, however, reduce his role to that of an area representative, and your person will not be able to play his part in an acceptable manner. Your real goal is to have your person near important clients and prospects to be able to respond promptly and efficiently to their needs.

Your man on the scene will have some very obvious duties. As your ambassador and legal representative, the person should have a power of attorney to represent the firm. In fact, if your client is a foreign government, there may be a clause in the contract which requires an officer, with authority to represent the firm, to be stationed in the country for the duration of the job. Your person should also have explicit power to conduct whatever business is needed to fulfill the contract and to provide for his own support.

An important point to remember: Your person will not replace your local associate or your legal agent (if one is required by law). Rather, the two must form an effective team, for it is essential that they be compatible and able to work as partners.

Together they must identify prospective clients and projects. They must locate the seat of power on the prospective client's staff and call on that individual regularly.

Each team member should understand each role and not usurp the other's place. The success of this relationship may depend in good part on the officer at headquarters to whom they both report. This officer should meet with them occasionally for frank and objective discussions. Both should be well informed of their goals, and their roles should be kept separate. Above all, there should be no grounds for conflict or jealousy.

A successful man on the scene might match the following profile:

- The individual studies local customs and traditions and learns to respect them. This sounds elementary, but local customs are often overlooked. One foreign firm had considerable trouble in North Africa because its resident engineer had given a gift of whiskey to a client's employee. When the recipient, a Moslem, was found drunk on the steps of the mosque, the blame had to be allocated, and the consultant was the logical culprit.

- The team member learns the language in a way compatible with personal ability. Arabic, for example, is a difficult language which most foreigners never learn to dominate. It may be far better to concentrate on some polite phrases to use when being introduced rather than to waste time trying to create a linguist out of a poor student.

- The team member studies geography and history and knows the importance of local and regional current events. In another strong culture, it is helpful to know about the religion and the traditions of the country.

- Your person is friendly with the client's staff in order to get "early warnings" on new projects. These friendships, often with local professionals, will offer ample opportunity for an exchange of ideas. This interchange will build credibility. In countries where age receives considerable respect, older foreign professionals will find their advice sought on everything, from cloud seeding to the use of sewage treatment plant effluent for irrigation. This may lead to new professional opportunities because of the establishment of credibility and trust. For example, someone in this category might be just the person to design a palace for the king! He and his family create an acceptable lifestyle and enjoy their exposure to the new culture.

Lest one forget what brought our man to the new post, it seems pertinent to suggest some routines that will enhance effectiveness. The gathering of industrial intelligence, or just finding out "what's happening," will be the greatest challenge. There are usually not many reliable published reports about projects, requests for proposals, tenders, or awards. Many things that are published in reports or periodicals are so stale that their main use is historical.

The best way to get information on projects is to develop a private network. Leads can be traded, rumors scotched, and competition identified by using one's own contacts to arrive at a consensus. The need for this help will be evident on the fact-finding trip, when languages, customs, and daily routines are new. This primitive method of gathering intelligence will pick up gossip and useless information like a giant vacuum cleaner, but it should be recognized and mastered for what it can produce.

Besides the client's staff, the following are potential sources of information:

- Your own embassy's commercial section
- Construction equipment and material importers
- Bankers
- Aerial photography and mapping companies
- Commercial travelers of all sorts

Before leaving for the new post, check the alumni records of your own university. Local grads from your alma mater will respect the "old school tie." In Riyadh, for example, many of the Saudi professionals belong to "The Berkeley Club," an informal group of movers and shapers who attended the University of California.

Luncheon meetings of international associations and chambers of commerce are often attended by local and expatriate businesspeople. Other contact points include tennis, golf, and sailing clubs. At these watering holes one will learn about "a hotel that Gulfair plans for Doha" or the fact that "Shaikh X sacked his architect."

Your man's success (and that of your company) can't happen without effective communications to headquarters. Telephone, telex, data links, cables, and courier services must be tested for efficiency and reliability. The most difficult aspect of communicating is the problem of establishing a timely and meaningful dialogue with the home office. As a start, messages from the field should be acknowledged and answered promptly. For reasons of morale, it is good practice to show the people at the outposts that they are not forgotten. Answer communications "in kind"—airmail letters by airmail, telex by telex, and telephone calls by telephone.

Language usage should be refined and ambiguity eliminated. The use of electronic "scramblers" and business codes is not usually justified. Codes lead to misunderstanding, because there is always someone who doesn't know the code. The fact that such things are available may be of interest if you have a job in a place where the client owns the telephone and telex system or if your CEO appears to suffer a little from paranoia. On the day before the proposals are due it is a bad idea to send pricing information to your agent who is in a hotel full of competitors. Otherwise, probably no one cares.

Negative reports are needed at headquarters just as much as positive ones, so progress of the marketing program can be evaluated. Your person should send weekly telex summaries of his activities and include an updated appraisal of the probability of success for each prospect being followed. The home office needs this information to plan a strategic assault on the most attractive projects. Now that telephone service has improved to state of the art in many countries, an alternative to telex is a telephone-recording device, connected to a private number at the home office and a similar one in the field. Tapes can then be sent during hours of low traffic and will be ready for transcribing when the recipient arrives at work, if the time difference is great enough. New model recorders transmit at such fast speeds that an entire proposal or request can be transmitted in an emergency.

Once communications are well established, the home office marketing manager should build up rapport with the "man on the scene." Backup material, sales aids, technical information, and personal items should be sent promptly to the foreign post. The need for a washing machine hose, a fuel pump, or a battery for a calculator can become a crisis of vast proportions in a place like Bluefields, Nicaragua. Aid of this nature will do wonders for the organization and will ease the psychological pressure on your person. A close relationship is essential and will make each person accessible to the other for important communications. The person at the scene must leave a trail when traveling and advise the home office of the spots being visited.

When annual leave schedules are made, your person in the field should be encouraged to call at the home office for debriefing. Such visits should not be charged to annual leave but be classed as business-related. (After a year in Lagos, Nigeria, or Guayaquil, Ecuador, your agent would rather be skiing at Vail than sitting in your office!) One or two days of discussion with management and project personnel could be effective. A formal, firm agenda for these meetings should prevail, to make the most of valuable information. Otherwise, the visit could deteriorate into a series of meaningless coffee breaks that do not accomplish much except provide a forum for horror stories from the front.

As your person gathers more contacts and knowledge of the foreign land, a role as regional representative may evolve naturally. If the firm's capacity is large, there may be limits to the opportunities where he resides. Big projects may take some time to develop to the proposal stage, particularly if an international lending agency is involved. If there are attractive market areas within a reasonable distance, the regional role is a logical step. It will help amortize marketing costs and provide good exposure—if the market measures up to your survey. It is a waste of time and money to search for opportunities where none exist or where the hotel lobbies are full of competitors giving away projects with "tied" financial aid. However, if the man on the scene lives in a place like Singapore, Panama, Abidjan (Ivory Coast), or Bahrain, it's possible to be within commuting distance to several good markets.

In most of the countries where your person may be stationed, the company will also have an associate firm, as discussed above. In fact, it is probable that your man on the scene will become a valuable member of the joint-venture organization. If the firm is coventuring with several local firms on a project, interesting, if not impossible, situations may develop. Your person should have been fully briefed in advance on the nature of the associate relationship and should be instructed so no misunderstandings arise. Assuming that the relationship with the local associate is mutually exclusive, your person is "stuck" with the marriage and has to make it work. The efforts will, in this case, be concerned with helping and strengthening the local organization. One can imagine that a role almost like that of a management consultant will be assumed. The possibilities are endless.

I recall a situation in Iran where our man became a combination chief architect, engineer, production chief, and consultant to the joint-venture firm. He apparently was responsible for huge improvement in quality and production of an eighty-person design office. This also resulted in a program of seconding professionals from our organization to the Tehran office, which was of mutual benefit.

In a similar situation our man became an informal adviser to the foreign associate, which frequently infringed on that person's main function—the marketing of joint-venture services. The relationship tends to become complicated, and no formula is offered for its structure. Perhaps the saying "What's good for the partner is good for the joint venture" can be applied to rationalize the situation. Unless it seems that your person has been made into an aide-de-camp of the foreign associate, such a condition should be allowed to operate until several accounting periods show that the investment is not worth the return.

Developing a working relationship with the associate's management and staff may be the biggest problem facing your person in the new assignment. The leader of the associate's organization—who probably is its sole owner or a family head—no doubt considers his own position to be equal to that of the chairperson of the board of the foreign firm. In fairness to the person on the scene and to enhance any chances for success, top management must take a hand in getting this relationship started properly.

The main reason for stationing your person in the market was to create a presence and to obtain contracts. The advantage of this presence can be used in many small ways to collect pieces of incidental intelligence. For example, after an informal network of sources has been put together, random routine visits should be made to drink some coffee and to exchange gossip. In a way, these visits are used to leave new brochures and to tell a prospective client about new jobs the home office is doing in his field. These people seem always to be interested in learning of another school plan, a hydro project, or a highway program.

During such brief visits, these contacts may want to "pick his brain" about technical matters, such as the selection of a mobile soils laboratory or some computer equipment. Your person's unbiased yet qualified advice will be most welcome. He might even be talked into doing some free consulting for an athletic or recreational facility or to give opinions based on experience, such as aerial photography for mapping land to be flooded by a new dam.

The opportunities for interchange of ideas are endless. They can provide good grounds for an exchange of local information. For example, from such sources one could learn that a World Bank team will be in the country to investigate new projects for which financing has been requested. If your representative can meet some of these people and pass the word back to the home office, the firm can be in a position to make a good presentation to the Ministry of Public Works. And by the time for consultant selection, your firm (and your associate) could be well on the way to the short list.

Contacts with the chamber of commerce and local businesspeople are also of value because hotel expansion, real estate development, and other private projects start slowly and can be tracked without great effort. Your person can act to bring the firm's name to the sponsor's attention—especially if it's possible to get the help of the local associate's staff.

Contacts with business and government people—not necessarily at top level—will produce surprising nuggets of intelligence during the "off" season when the top people may be away for vacations and underlings are more relaxed. Your person could be asked to visit a site for a new project or to criticize a project description or to look at the resume of an applicant for an adviser's position. They may seem unlikely occurrences, but all these things have happened to me on unhurried visits to government offices. They work very well if you can carry them off without being a nuisance!

Your man on the scene should be self-reliant even if housed in the associate's office. He should not be dependent on others for that which he needs to do as your representative. Middle management in many parts of the world cannot operate without daily instructions from the top. However, your person will be placed in an untenable position if subjected to the whims of bureaucracy regarding salary and expense checks, transportation, communications, and secretarial support. This is particularly true in the Middle East, where there are restrictive rules governing foreigners. It would be well to open a separate company bank account which your person can use in case of emergency. A crisis may be no more serious than the prolonged absence of the associate on medical leave, but when such events occur, a family-owned business tends to grind to a halt.

It is also a good idea to insist that your representative arrange for his own accommodations. Tastes and values differ where housing is concerned, and frequently this item becomes the most controversial detail of the entire foreign venture. A "man on the scene" looked at more than fifty apartments in Tehran before the local associate was convinced that the amount of money he had allocated for the expatriate's housing could not provide an acceptable apartment.

The office of your representative should be well equipped. Although many foreign firms have good office furnishings, the rule is that only the owner's office is adequate. A list of equipment, including office machines, should be agreed upon with the associate before your person moves. A microcomputer, a telex, and a telecopier would be valuable tools. It may be necessary to import them. Like the matter of housing, such items may require more diplomatic maneuvering than meets the eye, because the local associate's staff will likely resent any person being better equipped than themselves.

If the nominated person on the scene has limited overseas experience, the final selection should be carefully studied. Because of the size of the investment, it may even be wise to allow the executive's spouse to go to the new post on a fact-finding mission. If there are to be negative reactions, it would be much less traumatic to discover them now than later.

Training for overseas personnel is available from several capable sources. For example, The American Management Association (135 West 50th Street, New York, NY 10020) and The Business Council for International Understanding Institute (The American University, 3301 New Mexico Avenue, NW, Washington, DC 20016) sponsor seminars with emphasis on getting along in other cultures. These training courses are expensive and should be budgeted for the operation. Eventually, after suitable experience, the firm should be able to find an independent consultant to conduct in-house training.

Your person on the scene has an interesting and challenging assignment. No two individuals will interpret their roles alike. The goal is to market professional service contracts, to create a local presence, and to provide all the local ingredients for successful proposals. The establishment of an informal network to provide early warnings is absolutely essential. And perhaps last but not least will be the development of a home office communications system that will portray market conditions accurately to top management. If all these goals are met and demand exists for consulting services, there is every reason to believe that the investment will yield profitable contracts.

# CHAPTER 9

# QUALIFICATIONS

Organization and a "game" plan for gaining entry to the export market have been determined by the homework phase, the fact-finding trip, selection of associate and representation in the target country, feasibility studies, and budgets for projects in the chosen market area. Before approaching clients who are looking for consultants, it is important to have clearly in mind the well-defined project cycle.

A capital project usually starts when an individual identifies a basic need. It might appear that a project is born when wealth comes to an oil-rich nation. This is possible, but generally the need has been identified years ago by the project sponsor. A highway to the port city, an airport to handle wide-bodied aircraft, a water treatment plant, or similar improvement often undergoes extensive examination and study well before funds become available. The poorest countries have great needs for basic improvements, such as schools, hospitals, clinics, low-cost housing, and potable water. Such projects are being studied and evaluated for inclusion in future budgets, if there is any possible hope for aid from international sources. These "wish-list" projects are authored by dedicated public servants and government officials. It is my theory that a certain individual is the motivating force behind every important project. The consultant should try to identify this person as early as possible. Armed with the basic facts, the consultant can enter the competition for selection with background that may give a valuable advantage when making a presentation to the client's staff.

The project planning process may require a long time. For example, the World Bank cycle has the following eight phases, which altogether may consume a period as long as ten years:

1. Identification of suitable project
2. Preparation, during which the bank and borrower consider all aspects and issue a report (Some preparation reports are prepared by consulting firms.)
3. Appraisal by the World Bank team
4. Approval by the loan committee
5. Negotiation between bank and borrower
6. Signing of loan agreement–credit agreement and project agreement
7. Implementation—design, construction, and operation of project
8. Evaluation—completion report and independent audit

This well-choreographed procedure goes on for a long time. Persistent consultants can track it easily. The World Bank reports the status of its projects in a *Monthly Operational Summary,* published as a supplement to *Development Forum.* Anyone interested in international operations should subscribe to the *Forum,* available from the DFBE Liaison Unit, World Bank, 1818 H Street, N.W., Washington, DC 20433. The *Forum* contains official information about procurement opportunities available under World Bank, Inter-American Development Bank, Asian Development Bank, and African Development Bank and fund financing. The home office and your person on the scene must produce leads on international projects before they appear in the *Forum,* if the competition is to be overcome. However, any country which borrows funds from international lending agencies will advertise in the *Forum.* The notices will usually be in the language of the borrower, which may reveal more about the project details than a formal English translation. The *Forum* is considered by many consultants as required reading for background on important projects.

The World Bank itself does not very often engage consultants; the borrower does that. And the "Bank" staff takes a dim view of consultants who prowl the corridors of 1818 H Street, Washington, D.C., looking for project leads. Sooner or later representatives of such firms are advised in no uncertain terms to "expend shoeleather in a visit to the borrower's home country." Excellent advice. The selection and contract negotiation for World Bank–sponsored projects will usually be carried out at the borrower's headquarters, where the request for qualifications (RFQ) originates. Before a first trip is made, information about the project can be found in the *Forum* and the *Monthly Operational Summary.*

RFQs come from many sources. Private intelligence networks and visits by traveling partners, associates, and representatives to prospective clients should have uncovered most of the important projects advertised in the press long before publication.

The best and most satisfying RFQ is the one made in person by a client's representative who might say, in passing, "By the way, would your firm be available to design a 250-bed general hospital on that site across the road?" Or, "Your firm was a very close second on the short list for the port project. We know your qualifications so well that I believe you would stand a fair chance of being selected to design the military academy." A World Bank resident representative in the field, satisfied with your firm's efforts in his country, might say, "I hear a project like 'ours' is being studied by a team from the Bank, in Chile." These are real "requests for qualifications" even though they are not expected and are admittedly infrequent.

When members of "the old boy network" get together to talk about how they were selected, most agree that early warning is the key and that contract awards are usually made to firms who were aware of the opportunity long before it was published in the press. Sources of news about large projects are:

- *Development Forum Business Edition*
- *International Construction Week Newsletter* and *Engineering News-Record Magazine* (McGraw-Hill)
- U.S. Department of Commerce's *Commerce Business Daily*
- *New York Times*
- *London Telegraph*
- *The Wall Street Journal*

- *The Financial Times*
- *The Middle East Economic Digest*
- *The Economist*

It is still valuable to read the published material for the designated target markets, if only to learn where the action is and what the competition is doing.

The general consensus is that an interested firm will be aware of attractive projects well in advance, will have its market strategy finalized, and its qualifications ready for early submission once an attractive project is announced. The well-organized foreign representative will identify the person behind the project at an early date and will have a good idea of the design rationale and the funds available. This timely intelligence is not developed by "hit-and-run" missions from the home office, but must be cultivated at a slower pace by your man on the scene. Identifying the person sponsoring the project and keeping the prospective client informed of your firm's activities on similar projects in other countries is a subtle way for the local associate to assist in marketing.

The client may ask for general information in the form of brochures, samples of previous work on similar projects, and resumes of key personnel who might be assigned to the contract. If the items sent have not been selected carefully with an eye to the client's needs, the result can be the client's receiving kilos of unrelated material. Well-qualified firms committing that error are often eliminated early because the reviewers are unable to detect whether the firm is competent in the specific area of their project. "Smorgasbord" submissions are most often not understood by clients in developing countries, where professional firms are small or nonexistent. It is difficult for officials in such countries to conceive of a multidisciplined firm having a staff of a thousand. Even though a large firm may have strengths in many fields—highways, bridges, ports, airports, and environmental design—the client may prefer to select a specialist firm with a smaller staff which submitted material showing one or two projects similar to his. I have often had the role of adviser to a selection board on a World Bank project in which this situation has occurred. One of the board members, reviewing a pile of qualifications, would say, "Airports, harbors, roads, water treatment plants—how can one office know about all these things? We want an expert!" If you are being considered for a hydroelectric project, don't tell your client about great designs for wind tunnels. The prequalification response should be addressed directly to the features of the program at hand. Of equal importance, the client should *not* be told that what you will propose is an exact copy of a project shown in your brochure. Make certain the person understands that what you are showing in your prequalification documents are just good examples of past work.

"Truth in (your) advertising" can also be important to your winning a project. Because some firms worked on large projects employing many consultants, their qualification material shows scenes which include the work of others. For example, in these times, it would be difficult to supply a picture of the Kennedy Space Center on Cape Canaveral which shows only the efforts of one firm—yours. The prospective client gets confused by these claims—actual or implied—and can become skeptical. For example: A very important client, holding my volume of presentation material, asked in a humorous way, in front of a large group, "Where is the picture of the Titan launching pad? If your firm does not have one, you will be unique in this group we are considering. Only one firm designed the pad, but you all have pictures of it." We had such a picture. Someone else was selected.

The prequalification response should be addressed directly to the program at hand. If the client provides a set of printed forms, adhere religiously to the format. Resist the temptation to be creative; there will be time for that if you are selected. If there are no prequalification forms, model the reply along the lines of one previously submitted for another project financed by the same lending agency.

The local associate's name should figure prominently in the response, and his qualifications should be presented in the same format as yours. The local associate will often maintain that the client "already knows all about me" and that there is no reason to submit his qualifications. Resist this attitude politely but firmly. Foreign advisers and bank representatives will also examine these submittals, and the documentation must be complete.

If you have no local associate, perhaps it is a waste of time to enter the arena. There is certainly little hope in declaring, "If selected, we will associate with a capable local organization," a strategy that I have never known to be effective. The client thinks you should have had plenty of time to study the project and to choose a local associate, no matter how short a period was allowed to complete and submit the qualifications. And this is probably right. It is one more reason to select a local associate as soon as the decision is made to enter the market.

Be very careful in selecting the resumes of key people to include with your qualifications. In general, rapidly developing countries have very high regard for advanced degrees and long experience. Nondegreed personnel are rarely acceptable, even as construction supervisors. Gaps in employment are usually questioned, as they indicate periods when the person was not employed in the chosen field or was engaged in something that may not have been considered acceptable to the client. Candidates for project assignment have been rejected for these two reasons. Be forewarned, and resist the temptation to experiment.

When stating associations with specialists, care should be taken to review their availability, qualifications, and agreement to participate if you are selected. Long-standing associates may be out of business—or deceased. It is embarrassing to have the client notice the resume of a world-famous consultant in your qualifications who may also be included in the submission documents of a competitor or who might even be dead. This happened, only once, to me.

Making associations with other foreign firms may be self-defeating, particularly if they are capable of handling the entire project themselves. Clients have been known to split joint ventures and to select only one member of the team. Usually this is done to negotiate with the cheaper or weaker member. Fickle joint-venture partners should be identified and avoided. The situation could perhaps be averted by a carefully worded joint-venture agreement, but it would be much more comfortable to have a very loyal partner.

The qualifications should be presented in the exact format shown in the RFQ. No suggestions should be given for design criteria or for solving the big problems of the project. After all, the final scope of work has not yet been published, and it is not very professional to try to solve the problem before it has been studied. If you have some great suggestions for saving time and money, it is preferable to remain silent until a design contract is obtained. Certain more sophisticated clients, such as Exxon and Aramco, are allergic to remarks from consultants which are prefaced by "What you really need is —." Curb enthusiasm to present dramatic solutions to prospective clients until after the design contract is signed and the first payment is safely in your bank.

It seems hardly necessary to point out that professional qualifications for services of well-trained minds should be neat and professional. Yet sloppily, hastily prepared submissions, poorly printed on bad paper, have eliminated many firms in international competition. Poor use of the client's native language is another cause for rejection. One Latin American official, stunned by the bad Spanish in a consultant's presentation, said, "This document is like a beautiful woman dressed in rags." Don't jeopardize your qualifications for lack of proper appearance and good translation.

The covers and bindings of prequalification material should have a distinctive color. Graphics should be first rate and project photographs should be in color. The binder should be instantly identifiable when included in a stack of material from other firms.

If all this seems unimportant, remember that international projects attract *world-class* competition, and some of the European firms will use superb graphics, color photographs, and printing. Don't risk elimination because of a shoddy submission.

Certain points regarding prequalifications are mentioned with a certain risk of oversimplification:

- The legal name of the firm, the name and title of the person to be contacted (the CEO), and the street address, telex number, and telephone number should be shown in several prominent places. When the prospective client wants to contact you, a secretary should be able to find your address readily. The client may also want to send someone to make a surprise visit to your office!

- The material should be purged in advance of items that may offend the client. Rather than list examples, it is suggested that close attention be paid to the client's cultural background.

- If your submission includes pictures of key personnel, give your person on the scene prominent coverage. The prospective client will be proud to identify the one whom they will deal with when the contract is awarded to your firm.

- Include information about the local associate's staff and qualifications in the proper place. If the material can be reprinted so that it looks like part of the book submitted, the idea will persist that you are "real" associates.

- Deliver the submission just before the deadline. Send the package with one of your employees or by courier if there is any doubt about the mail system (there usually is!).

- Advise the client by telex or telephone that the submission has been dispatched and when it can be expected to arrive.

- Send a backup copy, as well as a personal copy, to your associate, so that the duplicate can be delivered personally if the original goes astray.

The dos and don'ts to follow when submitting qualifications include:

- Do plan an attractive document—binder, paper, printing, graphics, color photographs, and text should project an image of professional competence, innovation, and experience.

- Do remember that the sponsor has been planning the project for years and that it may be the biggest single event in his professional life. Put yourself in his place: What would you want to know about a prospective consultant?

- Do show enthusiasm and originality in presenting your firm's interest in the project. Tell about your firm's experience in similar projects, not only with a cold list of facts but also in concise, articulate terms. Mention previous experiences in the client's country or in similar cultural and physical environments.

- Do list names, addresses, and telephone numbers of senior representatives of satisfied clients whom the prospective client may contact for references. Choose these people with care, and ask their permission before listing them in the submission material.

- Do get the qualifications delivered before the deadline date. Do not trust normal mail channels. Send the package by courier, or have an employee hand-deliver it.

- Do arrange a way of getting the proposal through customs. (Proposals have been "lost" in customs, and your competitors know how to clear this hurdle.)

- Do preserve the format provided for submission of qualifications. The preselection committee will try to rate your group in comparison with all the others, probably using a matrix chart. Facilitate the scoring process.

- Do be specific about your role on the projects used as examples in the submission. If your contract covered a very minor part of a project, better to omit it from your presentation than to create a wrong impression.

- Do give thought to language problems. If the official language of the client is not English, edit the text very carefully to make certain it is understandable to a person who knows English as a second language. The foreign language text should be written by a trusted technical translator. Beware of translation bureaus.

- Do respect the diligence, tenacity, and intelligence of the client's selection board. Avoid routine, unimaginative, and carelessly prepared documents. If the submission is of poor quality, will your designs be any better?

# CHAPTER 10

# PROPOSALS

Once the qualifications are submitted, the client's selection board has the task of making a short list of firms which may present proposals. At least, that is the accepted way that consultants from industrialized countries would like to see the process unfold. In actual practice, procedures vary drastically. Some examples follow.

■ If the project does not involve World Bank or other international agency funds, the client may follow its own rules. In many countries this means bidding (priced proposals), bid and performance bonds, and award to the lowest bidder. Although the documents may sometimes say "lowest acceptable bidder," in the international market, the lowest bidder always seems to be acceptable.

■ If World Bank funds are used, the borrower's methods of contracting are fairly well scrutinized by the Bank and chances are there is a definite "scope of work." The short-listed firms are normally asked to present priced proposals. Although the Bank includes price as a suggested criterion in its 1981 *Guidelines for the Use of Consultants by World Bank Borrowers*

*and by The World Bank as Executing Agency,* that decision
is left to the borrower: "In cases where it is appropriate to take
price into account, except as noted in para 2.36, the Bank does
not recommend any specific procedure other than to emphasize
that price as a selection factor should be used judiciously and
cautiously and should never undermine quality or client/con-
sultant relationships" (p. 17, paragraph 2.35). If price is used
as a criterion, the World Bank recommends that the technical
evaluation and the price be studied separately, using a two-
stage system. Variants of this system are used by other lending
agencies, including the Inter-American Development Bank.
Theoretically, the price envelopes are not opened until the technical evaluation is completed. But staff members of international lending agencies are generally not as naive as the word-
ing in their published guidelines would imply. Borrowers often
take a dim view of restrictions placed on them in spending what
they regard as their own money, to be repaid someday to the
Bank with interest. After all, if the local bank has a mortgage
on your home, do you consult its manager about the color selection for your bedroom? Alas, one fears that sometimes the second envelopes may be opened before the technical evaluations
are complete. At any rate, it is almost certain that there will be
some negotiation with the low bidder, in areas of the world
where negotiation is an everyday practice.

▪ Private and corporate clients have their own contracting procedures which vary from a letter contract at a fixed price to a
cost-reimbursable contract whose documents are 5 centimeters
thick. Selection procedures vary, and generally the process is
fair but tedious and time-consuming. This is strictly an "on-
the-job training program." Any understanding developed while
working for a large corporation at home will probably serve you
well in dealing with a multinational abroad. After the first contract, the rest are easy to negotiate. Strive to get selected the
second time, too, so that there is a chance to recoup.

When a request for proposal (RFP) for an international project is received, regard it with respect. After all, isn't the purpose
of the marketing program to obtain RFPs and to develop an
acceptable "hit" ratio (percent of proposals accepted) so a backlog of contracts can be maintained? Having an RFP in hand
means that there is a good chance to be awarded a contract, so
the opportunity deserves everyone's best efforts.

The first step is for a partner or vice president to read the text of the RFP and to formulate proposal strategy. The following questions should be addressed:

1. Is there time to prepare a proper proposal?
2. Is all of the pricing information at hand?
3. Is it necessary or desirable to visit the site again?
4. Is there a special list of new requirements in the RFP which cannot be met and may automatically signal exclusion?

These questions may be difficult to handle. For example, in particularly large contracts like those at Yanbu and Jubail, Saudi Arabia, the project administrators refuse to entertain questions from proposers, despite their having made a special and long trip for that purpose. The administrator's rationale seems to be that there is no time to study the questions and then distribute the answers to all contestants before submission date.

There is usually too little time to prepare, print, bind, and deliver the proposal by courier to the client before the deadline. If much input is required from the local associate, the latter must send representatives to your home office or prepare the proposal in his office. For a large project, with a fee of several million dollars, for example, proposal preparation is costly and difficult. The challenge should be to make every proposal the best possible.

The partner or vice president in charge of the proposal should examine the request, make a cost estimate for preparation of the proposal, and get CEO or board approval for the effort. In the first place, the marketing budget should provide for labor and direct costs. Few requests for proposal should come as a surprise because projects are being "tracked" over considerable time. The first few days' effort on a new proposal will occupy the proposal manager and one or two aides taking the following ten steps:

1. The proposal budget, including the cost of delivery, should be approved by the CEO.
2. Copies of the scope of work should be distributed to the technical department heads—so that their manhour estimates can be started.

3. A proposal team should be named to work full time on the final fee estimate.

4. A situation room should be assigned as the team's headquarters for the duration.

5. The final schedule for submission of manhour estimates, direct costs, text material, printing, graphics, covers, powers of attorney, legalized documents, review, signature by CEO, and delivery should be determined. The schedule should be printed and delivered to all concerned. The important dates should be posted in the situation room and initialed as acknowledged by team members.

6. The person who will deliver the proposal and an alternate should be named. Passports, visas, inoculations, plane reservations, and hotel bookings should be made as soon as the two are nominated.

7. The associate should be given a copy of the RFP, his part in the proposal preparation discussed and finalized.

8. Copies of pertinent sections of the RFP should be distributed to legal and accounting departments and the company treasurer. If a bond is required, the treasurer should receive all the details and be asked to deliver the bond to the proposal manager on schedule.

9. A firm date should be established for the first (organizational) meeting of the proposal team.

10. Preparation of the proposal should be established as a top priority for team members, who should be released from all other duties for the duration, including travel.

Probably no organization exists which could conveniently stop normal operations and take the above steps in preparing an international proposal. But committed firms will automatically fall into a pattern of action to give proposals top priority without discussion. The idea is to train a team and to eliminate the roadblocks to good performance.

Not all requests are easy to understand. Some industrial-type proposals for coal mine development, petroleum production and refining installations, university campuses, and hospitals are presented to consultants as though the client has issued a challenge for a firm to solve its puzzle. In this case, the RFP, which may be in ring binders weighing 4 kilos each, with a massive load of flowcharts and "boilerplate," must be distributed to design departments for interpretation. If the consulting firm has no experience with a similar industrial complex, but feels at home with the design of the elements, a professional who can interpret the flowcharts should be called in. The professional can produce a written description of the process and daily operations activities to clarify the architects' and engineers' understanding of the design needs of the project.

After twenty-four hours, the representatives of the design departments should be assembled to report what they think the client wants and to finalize proposal strategy.

Ideally, the arrival of the RFP should not have been unexpected. Communications from the person on the scene will have alerted management of this possibility months ahead of time. The firm may have done other projects for the same client, so the preparation could be more like a routine event.

The client frequently wants to know how a consultant proposes to proceed with the design and when certain events will occur in the course of preliminary and final design. To meet this need, the proposal manager should assign a professional to prepare a narrative of the design process and an activities schedule, perhaps in the form of a bar chart or a modified critical-path chart. This will also be a good in-house guide for checking the proposal. The narrative text should be concise and to the point—covering only the design process. The proposal should contain no sales material because the marketing phase is over and the firm was selected as one capable of producing plans and specifications for the client's project. Of course, the proposal should reflect this ability and its resources to meet the client's schedule.

International RFPs may come from the following categories of clients.

## Types of Client

1. Privately owned companies
2. Governments
   a. Self-financed projects
   b. International bank-financed projects
3. Multinational corporations
4. U.S. government agencies

Each one of these groups requires a different proposal philosophy. The most difficult and unpredictable prospective client is most likely to be in the first category, although one may frequently regard all international clients as unreasonable. Typical attitudes and points of view can identify each of these widely diverse client groups.

**Privately Owned Companies.**    The finest client, or the worst, falls under the heading of privately owned companies. The big problem is to find out what professional services the client wants and how much it plans to spend for engineering and construction.

A person-to-person relationship at the highest level of the consultant's organization may be the only survival route. Chapters could be written on the perils of such contracts, but the watchword is—"Caution!" The scope of work for both design and construction should be agreed upon before design fee or project cost estimates are attempted. The best policy for the consultant is to perform all services on a cost-reimbursable basis until the client decides what is to be built. Next in order is a lump-sum fee, or a cost-reimbursable fee with a not-to-exceed limit negotiated.

The difficult private clients are easy to identify. Their offices are full of sets of plans and architects' renderings of projects that remain unbuilt. Probably, the architects and engineers who prepared the plans were never paid. Insist on advance payments by such clients so that you work on *their money.* Scopes of work must be tightly written, since these clients will want to make changes during design and construction without paying extra fees. In spite of the drawbacks, such entrepreneurs often become repeat clients after mutual trust is established.

**Governments—(a) Self-Financed Projects.**    Proposals to rich foreign governments are the most difficult to handle. Iran, Libya, Nigeria, Saudi Arabia, Iraq, Kuwait, United Arab Emirates, and Indonesia are good examples of countries in which projects are huge, risks great. Since project funds depend on revenues from export sales of oil or minerals, payments may stop or be seriously delayed when exports lag. Yet when there is a good relationship with the client's staff, a good local associate, and goodwill, these clients get high marks. Consultants from Europe, the United Kingdom, and the United States have done very well in Libya, Saudi Arabia, Kuwait, and Nigeria through both good and bad times. Political and financial risks were great, but the real internationalists insure themselves for risks, work on advance payments, and, in some cases, have withdrawn in time to cut their losses.

Proposals to such clients should be carefully structured to provide for monthly advance payments to be made in convertible funds or an irrevocable letter of credit. Risk analysis should be used and insurance obtained to cover worst-case scenarios. The cost of such insurance must be covered by the fee. Because of risk, profit margins should be on the high side of the scale. Obtaining legal and tax advice from international firms specializing in the geographical area is mandatory. While for some conservative firms such projects are in "no-man's-land," for experienced international firms they are routine and profitable business.

**Governments—(b) International Bank-Financed Projects.** Most attractive are proposals by a foreign government for projects with international financing. The "umbrella" provided by the presence of one of the international banks is reassuring, even though the consultant does not have a contractual relationship with the bank. The owner is the borrower and the client of the financing agencies. The bank's staff expect the consultant to conduct its own affairs with the borrower. The consultant files credentials with the international banks by keeping the World Bank's "DACON" computer program updated. The input that goes to the World Bank is sent to the other international lending agencies, such as the African Development Bank, the Asian Development Bank, the Inter-American Development Bank, and some of the regional funds. When a borrower inquires of the banks, it learns then whether or not any objection is made to the selection of a certain consultant for a specific task. The banks will review proposed contracts between borrower and consultants, and their engineers will review the consultants' designs periodically. The presence of an international lending agency is reassuring to a consultant because payments by borrowers and by the banks are prompt, according to their bureaucratic procedures.

In some instances consultants are employed directly by the banks. The African Development Bank, the Asian Development Bank, the U.S. Agency for International Development, and other sources of development funds lend to some borrowers who may not be staffed to administer a consultant's contract, in which case the bank not only selects the consultant but also negotiates the fee and administers the contract.

**Multinational Corporations.**   The large multinational corporation can be a treasured client for large, well-financed consultants with plenty of resilience. However, the organizational
structure of these firms will make one forget that bureaucracy
was invented in Greece and France and immortalized by the
U.S. Department of Defense. Aramco, Esso Research and Engineering, ARCO, Exxon, Intercor, Occidental Petroleum, and
Mobil are a few sterling examples of fine clients. Each organization speaks its own language, sets its own dress code, and has
its own system of selecting consultants. Contracts are usually
cost-reimbursable, and each company has its own accounting
methods which must be followed to express overheads and
hourly multipliers. Payments are prompt and in hard currency.
Engineering reviews are prompt, fast, and generally unortho-
dox. This class of client knows what it wants and is willing to
pay, thus you will have a fine client if you can live through the
proposal period, for there is a great deal of travel and negotiation at your expense. It is worth the effort, but there will be a
challenge, especially when the multinational client is an
energy-related company. That's because rapidly changing production requirements force many projects to be delayed or canceled and then revived. Moreover, production-oriented engineers frequently discourage innovation and architectural
refinement, reflecting their emphasis on production and function.

**U.S. Government Agencies.**   Contracting with U.S government agencies for their foreign work is not very different from
contracting for their domestic work. Projects of significant size
are advertised in *The Commerce Business Daily,* and consultant selection procedures are well known.

Being awarded a U.S. government design contract for a foreign construction job is a safe way for a consulting firm to get
started in the export market. Fees are not lavish, and it is easy
to lose money on a fixed-price government contract. But payment is prompt, and the scope of work is usually explicit. The
problem is that to qualify for government agency projects, one
must usually have overseas experience and be familar with the
language, engineering standards, and construction procedures
in the host country. A drawback is that if a firm is selected for
one large design contract in a foreign area, it will probably not
be selected for another significant contract in the same area for
several years. Many companies are competing for government

projects, and the policy is usually to spread the work over a large number. Smaller contracts usually go to U.S. firms who maintain design offices near the contracting agency's foreign headquarters.

The U.S. government is a demanding client. Because most foreign contracts are built by contractors of the host country, contract documents must be bilingual and plans must follow the format required by local practice. The first few projects attempted will be for educational purposes and probably offer no prospect of profit since fees are low and tightly negotiated. Very few consulting engineering firms can exist on this diet alone.

As the proposal takes shape, technical departments should have completed a manhour count and a list of drawings for each line item, building, or task listed in the scope of work. The proposal team will have completed its checklist of direct expenses, travel and printing costs, consultants' fees, subcontract costs, and all other items not related to manhours of labor. The CEO and the treasurer should provide overhead percentages to use for labor and general overheads. They must also decide how much profit will be added to arrive at a total fee. The fee calculation procedure will be the same as for a domestic contract, except for coverage of additional risks that by now have been evaluated.

When manhour estimates are prepared by technical departments for overseas projects, there is a tendency to "pad" the manhours because of fear of the unknown. This is especially noticeable in organizations which do not have a firm commitment to the export market. As a check on the manhour estimates, two or three alternate calculations should be made. For example, a careful estimate of the number of drawings proposed is made, and a cost per sheet calculated, using only the costs for design and drawing preparation.

Another guideline is a check on the design fee as a percentage of the cost of construction. Estimators can produce a budget type of estimate using square-foot costs for buildings and infrastructure. A judicious study of these estimates and a review of the fee calculation should indicate a consensus and reveal where the proposal may be out of line.

If the firm does not have accurate records on costs of completed projects, of course, there may be no guidelines. To compete internationally, such records are vital.

Eventually, the proposal may have to be cut down to size—sometimes ordered by executive fiat. This is one of the most difficult tasks a consulting engineer may undertake. The fee has to be adequate to do a first-class design, at the same time sufficient to provide a return on investment to the owners. Calculated risks must be insured. Moreover, the proposal has to allow some negotiating room, but manhour estimates cannot be reduced without consultation with the people who produced them. Close examination of the estimates must be carried out rapidly if this condition arises. It is not unknown for engineers to make very high estimates for design costs when they sense lack of management commitment or are unsure of the type of reviews to expect from a new client. Management must eliminate these fears. The proposal should contain a list of all the items to be provided by the consultant, such as:

1. Original drawings
2. Number of copies for each submission of:
   a. Concept studies
   b. Preliminary drawings
   c. Final drawings
   d. Sets of contract documents for contractors (and cost per set)
   e. Reduced sets of drawings
   f. Specifications
   g. Estimates
   h. Design analysis (if submitted)
   i. Foreign language or bilingual drawings
3. Trips to site during design period and cost of trips when required by client
4. Renderings of architectural drawings
5. Scale models of buildings and other project features
6. Construction schedules
7. Miscellaneous—such as copies of special studies performed during design and reports by outside consultants

The proposal should also list items that the consultant expects the client to provide in great detail, even though such a list was included in the RFP. After the contract is signed, the client may get a little vague about some of the data that it said existed. If the consultant has to provide these items or to work without them, there may be cause for an extra claim. At the very least, such deficiencies may be used as "negotiating currency" at a future date.

A major part of the proposal, apart from the price, is the *methodology section*. As suggested earlier, a narrative of the design process was started as soon as the proposal team was organized. Now that the proposal is in final stages, the team leader should edit the narrative and add items that have been discussed with designers. This methodology section will be very important in the selection process, and it should be very clear and definite about procedures. Thus if it is planned to send design teams to the country to identify cultural needs that will be incorporated into the project, say so in the methodology section. For example, it might be that you plan to build a model and test it in a wind tunnel to determine the effects of sandstorms on the building surfaces. Describe this effort. If a geologist is to be sent to the site to search for proper aggregates before concrete specifications are finalized, tell the client what you plan to do. This portion of the proposal may help justify your fee. It will also point out much of your firm's planned effort that the client may not suspect.

An organization chart for the design staff, naming the key supervisors, is a good exhibit to include in the proposal. Since it may be a long time before the signed contract is in hand, the title of the chart should not promise too much. Something like "Typical Staff Assignments" will suffice. Include resumes for key professional staff, but remember that international clients are interested only in the backgrounds of senior professional staff and management.

A modified CPM chart with time periods, but no dates, should be included in the methodology section of the proposal. After the preliminary and final submissions of working drawings, allow sufficient time for review periods. Depending on the client, these review periods may require presentations, so the cost of taking a small team to the client's office for the reviews should be included in the proposal.

If part of the fee is to be paid in local currency, it is prudent to discuss exchange rates and convertibility with your bank's international department. There are ways to lose all your profit if exchange rates vary during the life of the contract. A number of consultants have blocked funds in banks in places like

Nigeria. Cover these points briefly in your proposal, without being too demanding. The real test will come at the contract negotiation, and the proposal's chances should not be weakened by pounding on the table at the wrong time.

The final draft of the proposal should be "signed off" promptly by accounting, legal, CEO, and the proposal manager. Accounting should perform a numbers check on the fee proposal; the final fee should be cleared with the CEO. If the proposal is in a foreign language, the final draft must be carefully checked by an employee or associate from the host country, if possible. If not, the check should be made by an engineer whose native language is being used. The need for this is obvious, because significant differences occur from country to country, and the client must feel at home with your use of the local language.

The overriding task in proposal preparation is, of course, the fee calculation. The manner of presentation will have much to do with the selection, but the fee will probably govern. I have seen a public works minister pick up a voluminous proposal and demand: "Just tell me what page has the price!" There is a feeling that anyone on the short list could do a presentable job and that price is the only criterion for selection.

No ethical consultant should offer a fee that will not allow the best effort to be done, with a return that will permit the business to continue. Proposals must be screened for unnecessary effort and products that are not required. Experience gained on domestic contracts will be valuable in structuring "lean" proposals for foreign projects. Our attention, therefore, has been focused on areas which require special attention in making successful international proposals.

The proposal should be assembled, and the priced portion guarded very carefully. This security problem is simplified if the two-envelope system is used. The idea of keeping the priced proposal separate from the technical proposal is not all bad. In any event, keep copies of priced proposals to a minimum. If only one copy can be presented to the client, fewer prying eyes will be tempted.

The copy for your local associate should have the price section removed, to be delivered to the person in some secure way. The proposal should be delivered by hand by a reliable and responsible employee or sent by courier service. The delivery trip is one that every consultant can well afford. If the cost seems high, economize in another area, such as attendance at professional conventions or team marketing trips, but deliver the proposal by hand. In the United States, registered mail and private courier work well. In the international arena, private couriers or messengers must be used. Remember, the package that went to Tokyo instead of Riyadh could have been a successful proposal.

## Principles of Proposal Preparation

- Treat the request for proposal with great respect.
- Track programs and projects to avoid surprise when requests for proposals are received.
- Formulate an internal policy for timely response.
- Involve local associates in meaningful roles.
- Investigate the project background and the concepts of its sponsor.
- Include methodology that reveals full understanding of the design process.
- Propose a level of effort and compensation that will support a high-level design effort.
- Include messenger or courier delivery in the normal cost of proposal preparation.

## CHAPTER 11

# INTERVIEWS AND PRESENTATIONS

At some point in the marketing process, in order to become pre-qualified, short-listed, selected, or awarded a contract, there will be interviews and presentations. And following contract award, there will be presentations of preliminary schemes, feasibility studies, and final designs. Life in some of the international architectural and engineering organizations is almost like being on the stage. Every alert partner or project manager has a telescoping pointer at hand. The age of the interview and staged presentation is upon us.

It was not always thus. Selection in the international market twenty years ago depended on the efforts of the traveling partner. Given sufficient briefing and backup material, this peripatetic paragon would present anything, from a design of a sewage disposal plant to a feasibility study for a banana packing facility.

As projects became more sophisticated and complex, project teams expanded to include economists, planners, architects, and construction managers. One or two professionals can hardly do justice to the cause of explaining the team's approach to solving the client's problems. Where once a quiet chat with the senior partner would assure the selection board that the chosen consultant could handle the design, planned formal presentations are now required.

Other factors contributed to the evolution of the interview. In the first place, the architects and planners who have been added to the mix were raised on critiques and competitions. At architectural school they learned to stand in front of the class to defend their design concepts. (Along with this they learned a new language, called "architectural English"—but that's another story.) The planners are veterans of public hearings where they became skilled at presenting their work and defending sometimes controversial schemes. The teams now have members who can inspire inarticulate number-crunching engineers to new heights of articulate presentation.

Rapid technological development of graphic arts exerted quite an influence in making presentations more elaborate. For example, where once the speaker might show a few color slides, we now have computer-programmed six-projector slide shows, with taped musical background and commentary by a professional whose voice sounds soothing and vaguely familiar. Filmstrips simulating a ride through the project or presenting aerial views of the completed buildings by use of scale models are almost commonplace.

Forms of presentation often seem more like theatrical productions. Not long ago I took part in a staged presentation to an international client in which all key individuals on the proposed organization chart went to the podium and explained their respective roles and how they proposed to achieve their objectives. Each individual was equipped with a business card, with role title, in the colors and logo of the proposal's joint-venture organization. Sophisticated presentations are the rule, rather than exception, in the modern export market.

The program for a successful presentation has to be tailored to its goals. If the presentation is an introduction showing the consultant's background and interest in a new client, a "canned" program on slides or videotape may be adequate. But when the presentation to the client takes place in the last stages of selection, a very carefully rehearsed program with a live cast is needed.

Foreign clients usually want to interview, at a very minimum, the project manager, the project planner, and the architect. The extent of detailed information to be presented should be decided after much deliberation and a thorough study of the scope of work furnished to all the prequalified consultants. If the client's culture is new to your firm, be on guard. Under this condition, telling prospective clients how you intend to design their project will be deadly.

Plan and rehearse the presentation carefully. Get the timing refined so that you will use only about 90 percent of the allotted period. The client will appreciate that, particularly if the review board has more than one consultant on the day's program. We once made some points (and, incidentally, got selected) by shortening a presentation—the review team's senior member told us afterward that the previous consulting firm had upset the schedule by running over its time limit.

In planning the interview, bear in mind that the proposed project is well known to the client's staff. It may very well be the largest single contract they have attempted. Some of the interviewers may be the authors of the project you want to design. It would be poor strategy to give the board the impression that you think the scope should be revised and that your firm really knows what is best for them. Plan a positive presentation.

The interview team should be chosen with care. Depending on the nature of the project, three to six members will be enough to take to the client's country. The following considerations should aid the selection of team members:

- The leader should be able to commit the firm to naming personnel who will be assigned to the project and agreeing to delivery dates and the contract price (once the proposal has been made).

- The leader should be a competent professional in the main sector of the project—a graduate design professional with an established reputation.

- It will be helpful if this person is a good speaker and can lead the presentation.

- The project manager-elect should be able to "walk" the review board through the concept study, preliminary plans, and final design. This individual should have a good knowledge of the local environment and culture or be prepared to describe how the knowledge will be acquired when the contract is awarded.

- The project architect should exhibit familiarity with local architecture and an understanding of the ways the local culture affects the design.

- The client may be interested in the specifications, estimates, and contracting procedure. If that is true, one team member should be prepared to address local building costs, codes or practices, and availability of labor and construction material.

- The team should have an "equipment manager–traveling secretary" type who can manage logistics, handle travel arrangements, and fill in if necessary for a team member who has dysentery. This person should be in on the effort from the start, so that there is an awareness of what is needed and why it is essential.

- The local associate may be a valuable team member under the right circumstances. The international vice president should decide whether it is appropriate for the associate or your person on the scene—or both of them—to take part in the presentation. If the associate is comfortable with the role, incorporate him into the team and at least introduce your representative at the meeting with the client. It will be a great asset if your associate can be a meaningful member because perhaps no one else speaks the client's language.

Preparing for the interview in a foreign country may seem like a simple task. In my opinion, however, there is much to learn from watching the preparations of a traveling circus or a professional athletic team. The interview team should be just about self-supporting, except for food and lodging. If there are slide and film presentations, the projectors should be carried along. There should be no doubt about the voltage and frequency of the electric supply or the type of outlets. An emergency kit with European adaptors, multiple plugs, tape, fuses, fuse wire, extension cords, flashlights, transformers, extra projection lamps, slide holders (carousels or trays), and basic tools should be assembled. Many good presentations have never been given abroad for lack of a spare projector lamp.

If large photographs, renderings, and sketches are part of your show, some thought should be given to their display. One international architectural and engineering firm uses a demountable "wall" made of aluminum pipe and canvas, which can be erected in a presentation room to hold displays and a back projection screen. This system makes an impressive installation in a Saudi Arabian army officers club, for example, or in a client's office. There is much room for ingenuity and thought in preparing for the interview. No one on the team should need to say, "But I thought you brought the extra projection lamp." All this gear should be packed in metal trunks or wooden boxes for shipment, with due regard to the size of aircraft cargo hatches. Reservations for cargo space, as well as passenger seats, should be confirmed before selecting a carrier.

Slide presentations should be carefully edited to fit the known or estimated attention spans of the prospective client. The program should be structured in ten- or fifteen-minute segments, with the basic program planned to take not more than forty-five minutes. This allows time for questions and discussion. It also gives your client the option of extending the program, rather than subjecting you to demands to "speed up" or to being cut off summarily when the prince has to leave.

Every slide presentation should have a script, listing the numbers and titles of the slides. This script should be packed along with the slides, and a copy given to the presenter and the logistics manager. The reasons are obvious. The slides might best be packed in carry-on luggage so that if things get out of hand, a slide projector may perhaps be borrowed or rented when you get to Mogadishu, Somalia, but your baggage doesn't.

I am sure there have been some great presentations made in an impromptu manner by the legendary gurus of the design profession. Having been present at a few of these performances which resulted in contract award, I can be a witness to that fact. But for every such event I estimate there may have been twenty poor presentations and several where the hapless victims have been summarily chased off the stage. Every presentation should be carefully organized in a thoroughly professional way to project competence and understanding of local culture.

Besides formal presentations of experience and capacity, there is room on the program for a low-key presentation by the team leader about the design philosophy and the approach to obtaining the input of the client's staff. Some carefully chosen success stories from past experience may serve to convince the review board that yours is the only team they should select. Beware extemporaneous discussions "off the top" of someone's head. Beware unwittingly wading into delicate areas in unplanned discussions. Even seemingly innocuous trivialities may turn out to be sensitive politically or culturally. So it is prudent that even "extemporaneous" remarks be prepared and checked by your local associate. The following successful interviews illustrate the preceding points.

■ A presentation for planning a mining town in the interior of Colombia called attention to the goal of making the town attractive to the inhabitants and thus reducing employee turnover. The daily routine of the various levels of employee—supervisory, technical, and skilled labor—was set forth in detail, as well as the routine of the families. Amenities popular with the culture were to be provided for in the communities. The local style of architecture was emphasized, and sketches of tropical-style housing were presented. Members of the team with experience in planning, building, and living in company towns spoke in an "extemporaneous" manner to the client's group of seasoned international executives. Professional design experience and references were hardly mentioned, because these items had been covered in the prequalifications submission. Result: interview successful.

■ At an interview with a U.S. government agency concerning a military academy in a Middle East location, the architectural and engineering team was led by a senior partner of the architectural firm who was professionally renowned as a designer of educational institutions. This man's enthusiasm for designing the facilities to achieve the client's educational goal was almost boundless. He had selected, with our help, a number of slides of completed projects to present to the board. In the process of showing them, however, he got so enthusiastic that he entered into an unplanned question and answer session with the board. Speaking in a conversational tone, this famous architect captivated the audience, including his teammates. The formal program was aborted, and following the architect's portion, we reduced the balance to conclude the presentation within the allotted time. Result: interview successful.

■ An interview with the Ministry of Public Works of a Latin American country concerning a highway program came about while working on a similar design and construction project in Ecuador which was being financed by the World Bank. Visiting Bank personnel knew that our firm might be interested, and suggested that in view of our performance, the Bank "would probably have no objection to our selection" by the second country for its highway program. In due course, our firm was invited to an interview. Our team was small—only one of the senior partners, an environmental engineer who spoke Spanish quite well, and me, the proposed project manager, not truly bilingual but enthusiastic. The interview with the board of directors of the highway department, all of whom spoke fluent English, was conducted entirely in Spanish. The atmosphere was friendly but formal. The board asked me to describe my role as project manager in Ecuador, my background in their country, and how we proposed to carry out the project if selected. We were well prepared for this discussion and fortunate to have the background they were seeking. Facility with language and understanding of the culture and environmental conditions contributed to our selection. Result: interview successful.

- A Kuwaiti businessman with many interests wanted to talk about doing some design work for his headquarters. Besides being the world's largest Chrysler dealer, this energetic young jet-setter represented over three hundred foreign manufacturers in Kuwait. Meetings were arranged in VIP lounges in Rome, Paris, Zurich, and other places convenient for him on his travels abroad. Our man would "hold court" with ambassadors, jewelers, tailors, lawyers, and others, including consultants summoned to meet him between flights, usually late at night. In true *majlis* fashion each conducted his business intermittently in the presence of the others. Sometimes I felt fortunate to have ten minutes allotted me to discuss the scope of design for his latest commercial building, apartment house, or factory. In keeping with Middle East custom, my Kuwaiti client's way of selecting a consultant and a project was based on "free samples." He would ask us to prepare (at our expense) a number of schemes, renderings, and scale models until he found what he liked. At that point, he said, he would be prepared to commission our firm for the final design. At one of these midnight interviews, I decided to give the shaikh the bad news: "When one of your Kuwaiti customers wants to buy a Chrysler Imperial, you let him try it for a while. If the customer doesn't like the car, you put it back in stock and sell it to someone else." A consultant, I emphasized, could not put a rejected scheme back in stock to await another client. The effort represents a loss of time and talent, which are the only products a consultant has to offer. "I am sure you will be more interested and involved in your projects," I pointed out, "if you are charged a fee for our preliminary work. Under these conditions, we will not be wasting each other's time." The jet-setter got the message and agreed to a cost-plus profit arrangement for all preliminary schemes. Once approved, a fixed-price design contract would be negotiated. Result: interview successful.

■ Libya (before Khaddafi) was the site of many interesting interviews for selection. Perhaps the most unusual meeting took place when we made a presentation of the plans and construction estimates for various styles of housing designed for a new city. A reconstruction agency was appointed, headed by a former prime minister, to manage the project. The agency board of directors was made up of farmers and merchants, all of whom had lost their homes and shops in an earthquake. The fact that the board members spoke only Arabic and Italian governed the choice of our presentation team members. We usually fielded a team with two Arabic-speaking professionals and two who spoke only English and Italian. The presentations were quite elementary, because this group was unfamiliar with architectural drawings. Sketches, renderings, and scale models were used extensively. The board members liked to gather around the displays, and our engineers and architects would point out and describe the features in a very individual approach. Estimates of cost were shown in large numbers and letters—in Arabic, Italian, and English—in large flip charts, in Libyan pounds, Italian lira, and U.S. dollars. Sometimes even this approach required further simplification. When we were presenting the cost estimate, a heated discussion broke out between the council members. It developed that these farmers and merchants were having trouble relating the cost in local currency to anything of value. "What we really want to know," one of the board members asked, "is how many sheep are we talking about?" The common denominator was the value of a sheep, a camel, or perhaps a hectare of farmland. Future presentations to this same group were structured to equate as many items as possible to readily understood units of measure. Result: interviews successful.

■ Another incident highlights problems with selection interviews in different cultural environments. Our firm was engaged to study construction bids for the new city, to recommend award, and to make a proposal for the supervision of construction. The low bidder for the construction contract was a state-owned Polish company, whose bid was about 30 percent under the next lowest bidder, a very competent Italian contractor. Our analysis concluded that the Polish firm did not understand the project well and that it had no profit or contingencies in its bid. The need for "hard" Libyan currency motivated its low price, a fact which the Polish representatives freely admitted. The reconstruction agency board, used to negotiating for low prices in their daily life, could not resist the bargain. In fact, no matter how much I tried to explain our recommendation of the second bidder, they could not understand why I did not want to take advantage of the low price. Finally the chairman asked, "Are you reluctant, or afraid, to supervise a contractor from a Communist country?" My reply was that we had no fears, but we estimated that the agency would ultimately pay a price equal to that of the second bidder, because of claims and change orders. The construction contract was awarded to the Polish firm, and my company was awarded the contract for supervision of construction. Result: interview successful.

■ Presentations to multinational companies can be difficult. A large architectural, engineering, and planning firm was selected to design some small company towns in the desert. The scope of work was quite explicit, but that did not deter the innovative firm. A very formal presentation was made to the client, with about twenty senior officers in attendance, at a small auditorium at headquarters. The lights were dimmed, the taped music began, and the multiprojector slide show started. The presenter said something like "We have studied your needs and desires, and we think what you really need is this innovative solution which we propose." And on he went, describing the detailed changes to the client's proposed project. One by one the audience left the auditorium, and when twenty minutes had passed, there was no one in the room except the presenter and the client's project manager. Result: no contract.

Interviews and presentations are important events in the consultant's life. Selection often hinges on the image projected by the team and its leader. "If these people can't organize a good presentation of their own capabilities, how can one expect them to do a good professional job for us?" Clients are cruel—but they have their project at stake, perhaps the largest job ever attempted in their country, and they are looking for assurance.

After planning and design contracts are underway, the continuing success of the architect-engineer often depends on presentations. The examples cited have described successful and inept approaches used to win the client's approval and support.

It may be necessary to make presentations to heads of governments or high authorities in developing countries. Although this happens infrequently, it can be a traumatic experience as these two examples illustrate:

■ At Monaco, we planned a municipal project containing an auditorium for a symphony orchestra, a school of music and dance, rehearsal rooms, and a grab bag of public facilities (such as public baths) which needed a home. The project had no real scope of work—nothing was fixed except the site, which was too small. Sketch plans, scale models, and architect's renderings were made and delivered to a person nominated by the prince as an intermediary. The client, or his professional representatives, never met with us. We were told what the intermediary thought the client wanted and changed our presentations accordingly. After months of changes and waiting, the project was canceled. The client paid our fee, but there was no professional satisfaction in this remote relationship.

■ In Saudi Arabia our firm was short-listed for a classified (security) project, along with three other firms. All communications concerning the project took place in person and usually in the presence of the competing firms. We were given the scope of work and asked to compete for selection. Preliminary plans, sketches, and a scale model of the buildings and the entire site were to be presented to the client in Riyadh. Each consultant was given a separate room to install his exhibit, and on the appointed day we each made a presentation to the client's project manager. These presentations completed, the client kept us waiting for a few days before he announced that a selection board including several princes was being formed and that we would be notified of the final presentation. After several more days of delay, we were advised that we were scheduled for a 2 A.M. presentation to the jury of princes. At the appointed hour the jury and retinue appeared, complete with incense pot, two princes, and several generals. Our presentation was programmed for about forty-five minutes. The meeting started with no introductions but an announcement that the princes had a very full schedule (at three o'clock in the morning) and that the presentation should be cut to about twenty minutes. We started our slide show, with our architect presenting the project in English. Very soon a general seemed to become nervous, and he gave me the "double-time" signal to speed up the program. At the conclusion of the slide show, we invited the jury up to the site model for a guided tour of the project. It then turned out that the site was across the highway from the palace of one of the princes, and the jury got very interested. They spent almost an hour talking about the site. There was an unlabeled facility directly across from the palace, and our architect made an instant revision to the project. Instead of being a "wastewater treatment" plant, the unlabeled installation became a "water treatment" plant. We never did get introduced to the jury and have no way of knowing if they had been told our identity. Shortly after we returned to our home, we were advised that the project was indefinitely postponed. Great experience; unsuccessful presentation.

A competition is another kind of presentation that is very popular in Europe. Our firm entered two contests and won a prize in each. The first competition was for a headquarters building for Saudia, the Saudi Arabia national airline, in Jidda. There were first and second prizes in cash, with the first-prize winner also winning the commission to design the building. In addition, prequalified entrants were given two first-class round-trip air tickets from their home office to Jidda. (This accounted for the entrants from Australia).

The terms of the contest were well defined. The type, number, and size of drawings were spelled out, as well as the scales to be used. There was to be a design analysis in English and Arabic and a scale model whose maximum dimensions were given. We estimated our costs to enter and decided to take a chance. A competition team was selected comprised of the project architect with experience in design of structures for the Moslem culture and an Arabic-speaking engineer. A respectable entry was designed, and renderings and display drawings completed. A beautiful scale model, with shipping case, was built by our Italian model makers. We embarked for Jidda full of pride and confidence. The first shock occurred when we assembled at the Beirut airport. About twenty teams, identifiable by tubes of drawings and model cases, were waiting for the Jidda flight! Many of us were old friends or acquaintances, and we soon met all the competition who were on our flight. It appeared that many of the prestigious architectural and engineering firms in the world would be represented.

When we got to Jidda, we found that the exhibition of the entries would be in a new airport terminal not yet in use and that each entrant had been assigned about 60 square meters of floor in which to arrange drawings and model. We learned that there would be no oral presentation but that the jury would tour the hall on a certain date to judge the entries. After a week on the scene, our entry was awarded second place, tied with another American firm. The first-place winner, a small Italian architectural office, had submitted an entry that was a model in gamesmanship. Practically complete working drawings for the curtain walls of glass and asbestos cement panels, the doors and windows, and the interiors were displayed. These drawings, apparently furnished by suppliers, were complete with specifications. It appeared that the project could be built from the documents on display. We learned much from this competition. The money, from tying for second, may have paid 25 percent of our outlay. Presentation unsuccessful, but great lessons learned.

We won the second competition. This event was a great stimulus to the success of our firm in the international field and was a turning point in the firm's development. A strong earthquake in Libya virtually leveled a town in a rich agricultural area, killing three hundred and leaving thousands homeless. The country was entering into the oil-producing era, and the newly rich government decided to build a new city at a site selected by a team from UNESCO. An international competiton was conducted, with a jury of professionals from the Middle East. Our firm was already working in the country and had some current knowledge of the environment. The competition came at a time when professionals were available to work on the design, and it was decided to make a significant effort with the hope of getting the attention of a prospective client. The jury selected our entry unanimously, and as a result the firm was selected for a number of design and supervision contracts after the master plan was completed. Making the presentation of the scheme was a team fluent in Italian, with some Arabic-speaking members. The plan paid attention to the lifestyle in this farming community, and many hours were spent at the site studying traditions and customs of the people displaced by the earthquake who would be the future inhabitants. The ensuing design projects provided a backlog for our Rome office for several years.

The presentation philosophy was based around the idea of preserving culture while introducing public health, electricity, schools, a hospital, refrigeration, and other modern amenities and services the society could now afford and would tolerate.

Presentations were made with due attention to the conservative social climate and were well received.

There are special clients in the international market who follow stereotyped forms of selection interviews. These include the U.S. Navy Facilities Engineering Command and the U.S. Army Corps of Engineers. The Navy selection board process is quite formal and may have all of the trappings of a court-martial. Preselection methods are normal, the same as is used for domestic contracts. The short list is formed from a study of experience, organization, and previous performance. The selection board is usually headed by a contracting officer of command rank, which is heartening because this person can make decisions without leaving the room to consult higher authority. Because the Navy has a great interest in methodology, its selection boards normally include civilian engineers with design backgrounds.

Presentations to this sort of client must be well planned. Experience on similar projects should be well documented. Usually the project has a well-defined scope of work. If the scope is indefinite, there may be an item in the RFP for a design study to finalize the scope. The presentation should be carefully timed and orchestrated, and 20 percent of the scheduled interview should be left open for questions. Since foreign projects are being discussed, there will often be a person on the selection board from the site. Determine who this person is, early on, and address that individual to ensure that knowledge of the environment is conveyed to the selection board. The formal courtroom atmosphere is sometimes an advantage to a well-prepared consultant who is not intimidated by the proceedings.

Presentations conducted by the U.S. Army Corps of Engineers are sometimes similar in format to Navy proceedings but are not as predictable. The Corps' philosophy seems to imply that its civilian engineers take a greater role in selection and that the contracting officer is only concerned with budgets, schedules, and legal procedures. Selection interviews tend to be less formal than those of other government organizations and are at the same time more inquisitive. In this age of litigation, the board frequently wants to know whether there are any lawsuits pending in which your firm is a defendant. Since large consultants always seem to be defendants against nuisance and accident claims, these questions sometimes tend to disrupt an interview. Be prepared for them, and let your lawyer talk to theirs, if necessary. Again, careful preparation and execution of the interview proceedings will pay dividends. Board members selected by the corps probably attend more interviews than any other similar group, and they tend to have a low threshold for lack of candor. Keep the interview factual and emphasize past performance on similar corps' projects.

The proposed project manager should be on the interview team and should have a grasp of the special requirements for design and construction in the host country. If the interview is held in the Frankfurt, Germany, office of the Corps, lack of familiarity with German design and construction practice will surface early in the interview. The team should be prepared to address this subject.

Interviews with the Navy and the U.S. Army Corps of Engineers for foreign projects require very thorough preparation because competition is so tough. The fact that one has reached the final selection interview is in itself a sign that the board thinks your firm can do the job. In fact, the letter of invitation to the interview frequently says, "Your firm has been selected as one which is capable of performing the services described"—etc. So the interview is the final stage, and it should be regarded with respect. The board is really looking not for a reason to select as much as for one to reject your firm. Tread lightly on comedy, arguments, and defensive attitudes. Radiate professional competence and integrity. Stick to the program, allow time for questions, and get off the stage when your act is finished. Do not engage in sales efforts at these meetings. If another firm is selected, the good impression you have made may pay off on the next selection. Remember, if you are selected, there may not be another job for a long time, because Congress wants the work passed around to all its qualified constituents.

The following situation-tested guidelines, drawn from my experience, are for the reader who wants to maximize the success of presentations and interviews:

- Presentation techniques are changing rapidly with the development of new graphics tools.

- Videotaping, teleconferencing, specially prepared films, and exotic scale models will be used by your competition. Consider updating your presentation technique for appropriate prospective clients.

- Concentrate on methodology. The client wants to know what to expect if you are selected.

- Introduce the project manager (PM), who should play a meaningful role in the meetings. The client's acceptance or rejection of the PM will have a large bearing on your selection.

- If your firm has experience in the culture and environment, emphasize this knowledge. If experience is lacking, show how you propose to acquire it, before the question is asked.

- Do plan the presentation very carefully.

- Don't engage in sales campaigns at interviews.

- Do use the best graphics your budget will permit.

- Don't "talk down" to the client's staff.

- Do involve your local associate as a member of your team.

- Don't leave the project manager at home.

- Do radiate professional competence, awareness of cultural differences, and integrity.

# CHAPTER 12

# SUCCESSFUL NEGOTIATIONS AND STRATEGIES

Along with airplanes, computers, and communications satellites, consulting professionals have "discovered" negotiations and negotiating strategy. Every business-oriented publication has an article about courses one can enroll in to learn how to negotiate through to instant success. But negotiation has been around for a long time. Phoenician and Yankee traders knew about negotiating. Pilgrims negotiated with Indians; farmers negotiate produce prices; and police negotiate for hostages. In the export market, consultants will have to negotiate their contracts.

Modern professionals seem to be ambivalent regarding the existence and extent of negotiation. If you were entering the engineering profession during America's Great Depression, about the only option open to negotiation in an employment interview was the date for reporting to work. Negotiating was something reserved for labor unions. Consulting engineers did not negotiate. Their proposals referred to fee scales set by the learned societies, and (theoretically) every consultant used the same scale. It was agreed that consultants would refuse to bid on engineering contracts. This position proved to be untenable in the export market, and by the 1960s a real dichotomy existed. U.S. consultants were bidding openly in the international market for design projects financed by international banks while trying to hold to a domestic system involving selection first, followed by fee negotiation between the selected bidder and the client. The ethical standards of the profession have been restructured—with "help" from the Department of Justice—to accommodate these developments. The laws of many cities, states, and countries now require that contracts financed by public funds be awarded to the lowest bidder.

It may appear that this capsule treatment of such a complicated subject covering a fifty-year period is pretentious. Surely the matter merits wider and deeper discussion. But this text is not the proper forum. My goal is to provide guidance to professionals dealing with other cultures and changing conditions. Survival in the international marketplace depends on understanding business practices and the motivation of clients and associates. No programmed operation plan exists for every situation that will be confronted when exporting professional services. By provoking original thought, this book should, as previously stated, eliminate the "gee-whiz" factor, reduce surprise, and prepare an international consultant to succeed.

At home, negotiations are all around us. Sports figures, politicians, entertainers, and professional employees negotiate for salary, position, and perquisites. Yet when we cross over into other cultures, the discovery that negotiation is so important tends to come as a shock. Cultural differences have been described as "the things we don't understand about the other side." Be prepared to acknowledge that negotiation will be of prime importance in developing countries. It would be safe to say that the need for negotiating increases in direct relation to the distance from the home office. In the Arab culture, for example, compromise and negotiation are fundamental. Moslems, who are polygamous, are in a constant state of negotiating their status and fair treatment. A Libyan friend told me that he reserved Thursday afternoons for negotiating sessions with his family! In stores and markets, nothing may have a price tag— prices are open to discussion. In Latin America and southern Europe, shopping is bargaining. Even the most elegant lady will close her chat with a shopkeeper by asking for "a little discount." Will something be thrown into the bargain to sweeten the deal? Sometimes the negotiating seems to be more an art form than an actual desire to lower the price or raise the quality significantly. If you don't ask, you don't get it, so why not ask?

The consulting engineer entering new markets should be alert to the importance of a good negotiating position.

When foreign advisers are involved in consultant selection, the situation becomes more complex. In the Persian Gulf States, for example, it is not uncommon for clients to have Egyptian, British, American, and Palestinian technical and financial advisers. Added to the mix are usually native engineers, recent graduates of prestigious universities, who are actually in training to become high government officials. Such a team will present a tough challenge to a consultant who underestimates the importance of preparation for negotiating sessions. Besides their native experience in such dealings, these people are motivated by a need to prove their worth to their employer. Since they know what the client considers important in the project scope, these advisers and technicians are apt to discount a consultant's emphasis in certain areas of design. In this case, it will be very helpful to arrange a discussion of the scope of services before discussing the financial details of the proposal.

When a proposal has been made on an indefinite scope of work, the consultant should be well prepared for negotiation. A detailed execution plan and methodology statement should be taken to the bargaining table, and in every area of disagreement, the intended scope of work should be justified. If the effort is not desired by the client and can be eliminated or reduced without jeopardy to the quality of the professional effort, there may be a way to reduce effort and fee without losing face.

The negotiation format will vary widely between classes of clients, as outlined in the following paragraphs.

- Private contracts will require almost continuous negotiation before good levels of trust and confidence are established. Cost-reimbursable arrangements are much preferred until the concept of the project has been developed and a tight scope of work established. Since there is not much doubt that the client has an innate right for a change of mind, this sort of reimbursement is fair to both sides. In addition, there may well be a higher authority lurking in the wings, such as an older brother, a prince, a wife, or a trusted adviser. Be prepared for this when the client says, in a moment of good fellowship, "By the way, my friend, how about adding a two-story penthouse?"

- Self-financed contracts with governments will of necessity be negotiated. Being the lowest-acceptable bidder means only that one has been awarded the right to compromise. There have been cases where the consultant was able to increase the scope of work and the price at such a negotiation, but that rarely happens. The proper approach is to restudy the scope of work to justify design effort or to agree on a decreased number of man-hours. But if the client is not equipped to handle these details for lack of technical staff, negotiation will be difficult. It is important to remember that one does not reduce price without reducing effort, unless there has been a misunderstanding in the original estimate.

- International bank-financed projects may not require much negotiation. If the client has had long experience with the lending agency's policy and the design fee falls near the norm for similar projects, negotiations may turn out to be only a face-saving formality for the client. Don't count on it! There seems always to be someone on the staff who doesn't want foreign consultants or who supports another of the competing firms. In this case, the opponent inwardly acknowledges defeat but refuses to give up without a fight. So be prepared to make a show of conceding on some minor point that will reduce effort. Some tactful discussions with knowledgeable people about fees paid by the same client on previous engineering contracts may be helpful. This information should be available to the public, and your local lawyer and associate can help uncover it.

- Multinational corporations normally negotiate engineering fees in a very civilized manner. Their staff, in contrast to that of other clients, probably knows exactly what kind of design effort is required. When scopes of work are not definite, cost-reimbursable contracts will be offered. The negotiation will take place with discussions of general and administrative overhead charges, travel and vacation policies, profit-sharing plans, and other such items. Since the people you will be negotiating with represent profit-oriented corporations, they will accept a reasonable profit figure. The areas that are, however, inviolate for them include quality, flexibility, and deadline dates.

- U.S. government agencies engage in their own form of negotiation, which can be as difficult as that of any foreign client. One usually negotiates with a second or third level of the hierarchy, who has been instructed when to say "No" but not when to say "Yes." Design fees are keyed to the federal legislative ceiling of 6 percent of construction cost for preparing plans and specifications. The key is to determine that the government's construction cost estimate is reasonable and that your fee estimate is properly detailed. Mutual trust and respect are as important here as in the developing countries.

- Another kind of negotiation which goes on with all the above clients should be recognized: The frequently subconscious attitude of evaluation and testing of the opposing side—consultant or client—during daily contacts. Many consultants do not appreciate the significance of this culturally motivated attitude, discussed throughout this book. Arabs, for example, seem to be intent on one's reactions as may be signaled by eye movements. Greeks have a strong heritage of curiosity about the possibility that a stranger is an enemy. Latins like to know the extent of one's emotions. Far Easterners will try to draw out their adversary without disclosing their own weaknesses. Because this sort of "negotiating" goes on in the international market, one should be prepared for it and, while enjoying the experience, can enhance a personal evaluation of the client's representative.

Since negotiations are almost inevitable, good preparation by your team is very important. Dress rehearsals, role playing, videotaped critiques, and coaching should be considered where appropriate. The following are some of the points which should be considered in the preparation of the team:

- *Power of Attorney.*  In almost every international market it is a custom and requirement that the persons authorized to speak for the consultant have a power of attorney, in the official language of the client and duly authenticated by their country's foreign office and the client's consulate. The document should contain board resolutions authorizing the individual, in broad terms, to do all the things that must be done to enter into the contract and to conduct the business described in it. The authentication procedure is long and tedious, so it is best to provide powers for more than one individual, in case of a substitution.

- *Team Organization.*  The negotiation team should be organized and managed by the leader. The leadership position must be maintained. But when specific points arise, the leader should designate the person who will speak for the team. Lawyers and accountants should not debate technical issues. Overhead percentages are better left to the accountant. The team leader should stay out of the bickering in order to keep the option of being called on to compromise or make demands in the name of the organization.

- **Dress Rehearsals.** It may be useful to organize a mock negotiation, complete with an opposing team. If videotaping is convenient and the contract is important enough, the session could be taped and reviewed. Your group may not be ready for this innovation, but its members should be prepared.

- **Negotiating Garb.** Although clothing is not of great importance, some thought should be given to appearance. Conservative western dress is generally acceptable, and the client will feel at home with you if shown this respect. As a rule, dress as the client might when the latter comes to visit you.

- **Jet Lag.** The disastrous effects of jet lag on the decision-making process have been well documented. Arrange the meeting schedule and your flights to arrive a day or more before the first meeting. Many important conferences have been ruined because someone on the consultant's team could not control his temper under fire. Jet lag is a contributing factor, and its effects should be known, respected, and avoided.

- **Eating.** The gamesmanship factor always seems to surface in international negotiating sessions. Meetings are scheduled late at night or just before what we consider mealtime. The other side never seems to consider when your team eats or sleeps. Feed the team early when it appears that normal mealtimes will be missed. In Ecuador, the client always scheduled meetings which lasted from 5:30 P.M. to the late hours of the night. It became routine to eat dinner before these meetings. Our team had great staying power when the other side was getting hungry and restless.

- **Organize Details.** Do not take briefcases full of uncataloged material into delicate negotiating sessions. Each person should have his own reference material and a copy of the proposal. One of the team should be official recorder and take official notes about agreements made with the client for any increase or decrease in fee or changes in the scope of work.

- **The Picador Principle.** Negotiating strategy should be studied thoughtfully. In the Middle East there is a tendency to wear down the consultant's first team by letting them deal with minor staff "picadors" having no authority. This situation should be recognized early. At the minimum, the team leader should withdraw, to let the picadors deal with the least senior people. The client will understand this reaction and respect it. The U.S. Army Corps of Engineers also uses the same tactics, reserving two or three higher levels of authority to bring into play if negotiations reach a stalemate. It is well to consider this possibility and not to use all your "negotiating currency" or trump cards during the first sessions. Let *your* picadors deal with *theirs.*

- *Pricing Policy.* When a priced proposal is submitted, the possibilities of negotiation should be anticipated. If there is a good prospect that the client will be looking for reductions in price, the proposal should be structured accordingly. This is an area where we sometimes confuse cultural differences for dishonesty or unethical practice. "Negotiations" normally do not mean that the client will unilaterally raise one's fee. Negotiation means compromise, and the client will expect more effort for the same fee or a lower price for the same amount of effort as proposed. The basic rule is not to reduce fee without a corresponding reduction in effort or services. This noble principle should govern all negotiations for consultants' fees.

Accordingly, one should be prepared. There may be some very strong financial or legal reasons why a client cannot approve the design fee proposed. The consultant should analyze the proposal and make one or more drafts of it, trimming services and fees by not more than 5 percent in the first option and 10 percent in the second. There also must be a final proposal— the "rock-bottom" price and service version, which management has approved as an offer which cannot be reduced. A word of caution: Electronic word processing equipment makes the mechanics of producing original copies very simple, and the team leader should keep these unsigned proposals under lock and key until the time comes to use one of them.

This pricing approach is difficult for some professionals to accept because it may be confused with unethical practice. No compromise with quality or design principles is suggested or intended. The idea is to tailor the scope of professional services (manhours of labor and direct costs) so that the fee can be adjusted to meet the client's budget. There are many ways to reduce fees without compromising design effort. If this is your first project with a certain client, the latter may not have the faintest idea about the number of sheets of drawings, pages of specifications, or manhours of design effort, checking, and analysis that you propose to furnish. If there has been any past experience with European engineers, your client would be accustomed to electrical and mechanical design being furnished by vendors and contractors. So, for example, the client may think your fees are excessive in these areas. Presentations should explain in detail what it is intended to be furnished. There are many areas similar to the mechanical and electrical design which should be well understood before proposal preparation and negotiations begin.

It can be very helpful to review a full set of contract documents for another project designed for the same client by a consultant from a different continent—Europe, the Middle East, or Asia. Check scales, details, number of design drawings, number of shop drawings, estimates (quantity surveys), and specifications. Compare these with what you would normally furnish the client. Proposals and negotiation strategy should be structured with such background information on competitors.

**The Local Associate's Role.**   The local associate can be a very helpful adviser during proposal preparation, presentations, and negotiation. The associate's role will be defined differently in each association and each contract. A number of examples from my experience illustrate the variety of roles that the local associates may play in these proceedings:

- IN LIBYA.   In Libya, an associate was of great help and comfort in coaching the negotiating team, helping them understand the local culture. Although he preferred not to take part directly in the negotiation process or the technical part of the contracts, his sage advice was priceless when dealing with the client. From him I learned that our Moslem client was conservative to the nth degree and uncompromising in any cultural matter. This associate warned me not to be intimidated when our client acted shocked at our first fee proposal, that a 4 or 5 percent reduction in scope, effort, and fee would probably be accepted if I acted very reluctant and took sufficient time in preparing the alternate proposal.

- IN NIGERIA.   The contract for design of a university in Nigeria required that a large portion of the design be shared with local associates. The project was large, but the local firms were generally so limited in capacity that many associates were required to produce the local percentage of effort demanded by the tender documents. Bargaining with this unorganized group of local consultants promised to be more frustrating than contract negotiations with the prospective client. After hours of haranguing, our Nigerian associate, Chief Oku, stepped into the meeting and, asking permission, proceeded to beat the team into cohesive shape with his wonderful persuasive command of English and his best public relations manner. Amazingly, this group became a team, and the chief kept the members happily in line with our policies.

■ IN SAUDI ARABIA.   In Saudi Arabia, the outsider will be at a complete loss without a strong, well-placed professional associate. At present the law requires foreign consultants to be associated with a local professional; there is no alternative. But because of the political structure of the kingdom, just any professional will not do. Status and family must be evaluated, as well as professional standing. Increasingly, the Saudi professional ranks are swelling with well-prepared, intelligent engineers, architects, and planners, who are motivated to serve their country. Such an associate is invaluable and deserves a proper share of the decision-making and management role. In negotiations, this associate will not want to enter into the discussions with the client's "picadors." It comes down to a matter of pride. Your man may have been a university classmate of a member of the client's staff, a member of his family, or a colleague on the university faculty. Rather than take part in the negotiating, the associate will want to assume the role of coach. When the negotiations were going against us, our associate arranged an informal meeting with the client, the director of the agency, who had been his classmate at Berkeley. We had an opportunity to state our position, and the next negotiating session went very well. We had gotten out of range of the picadors.

■ IN PANAMA.   In Panama, a surface evaluation will equate local professionals to those in the United States. Equal in education, dress, language facility, business acumen, and material values, Panamanian professionals will lull one into a false sense that conditions there are equal to those at home. Yes . . . and no. Panama is a special place with complex political and cultural influences which the local associate understands very well. The local professional will know when to withdraw gracefully to return to fight another day. Lessons learned in Panama's small arena have benefited many consultants. Our Panamanian associate evaluated prospective joint-venture opportunities, and his knowledge of the competition helped us avoid wasting our efforts.

Much written about the art of negotiating will be of value to the international design professional. It is dangerous to think that a consultant's problems are entirely different from those of others, because that is only partly valid. In short, knowledge gained from many sources will aid in dealing with other cultures. Some principles established from lessons learned in negotiating contracts for professional services with foreign clients will provide guidelines and food for thought:

- *Stay Cool.* Probably the ability to maintain one's composure in the face of opposition, disappointment, and ignorance is the most difficult to develop. Probably other cultures will need some thousands of years to develop the calm attitude that characterizes the Chinese, Korean, or Japanese negotiator. But we can try to maintain a sense of humor and be gracious when the client wants a 50 percent price reduction or delivery of plans in a few weeks. Breathe deeply, think of waterfalls, or something that will make you smile, and try to keep quiet. Change the subject, or produce a modest present for everyone, but keep cool. Angry people can't negotiate. Don't send any signals that betray this weakness. If members of the proposed team have this defect, leave them either at home or back at the hotel during the sensitive discussions. Keep *cool.*

- *Establish the Seat of Power.* Find out who has the last word in the approval process, and get your case to that person. This is easy to counsel, difficult to achieve. The goal is to find out who will make the final decision and to make sure that individual knows the whole scope of your proposal. Perhaps the only one who has access to the power is your associate. If so, the latter must be fully briefed in order to talk knowledgeably to the power without your presence.

- *Reserve Some of Your Power.* Don't send the leader into the fray with the picadors. Sometimes this can be accomplished simply by excusing the team leader, who may then "call on the minister," "visit the embassy," or have a slight case of indigestion. Refrain from telling your client that certain decisions must be cleared with higher authority back home. After all, since you have presumably produced a power of attorney allowing you to negotiate, such a remark ruins your status and may cause the client to suspend the meetings. Actually, the scenario requires that both sides be represented by equal power. Faced with such a dilemma, the team leader should ask for a private appointment with the power and withdraw until such a meeting is held. Obviously this move may make some enemies at the picador level and should be reserved for serious deadlocks. The leader should avoid the appearance of intimacy with any of the client's staff, until the contract is signed.

In Asia value is placed on maintaining status and face. We negotiated all day with a Taiwanese client's team headed by an alert, white-headed senior person, who used an interpreter and professed to have no English language facility. After settling the deal, on terms which were considerably at the low end of our scale, the "power" came to my office to use the telephone. When the interpreter left for a moment, I tried to entertain the "old man" by showing him some of the amateur photography that was displayed on my office wall. "And this," I said very slowly and distinctly, "is the pond in front of my home." In perfect English he asked, "How far is your home from here?" He had not said a word of English all day. That's "cool": power reserved, very skillful negotiating accomplished, and all apparently according to a scenario. Another lesson learned!

- **Recess to Regroup.**  If negotiations tend to get off course, the leader should ask for a recess—time out to caucus and reconsider what is going on. It is not unreasonable to ask for a day's delay so telephone calls to the home office can bring in new strategy. Better telephone than telex, for a number of reasons, but remember that in some countries and under some regimes, communications are not very secure. In a North African country, a consultant was taking an early evening stroll in the hotel grounds when he heard his own voice coming out of a basement window. One of his calls to the home office had been taped, and someone was trying to figure out if he was a security risk!

- **Analyze the Client's Motivations.**  Try to determine what motivates your client. The person may be governed by some restraints that are inflexible. For example, during my effort to collect fees that had long remained unpaid, I was called in for "discussions." The client felt we should reduce our fees because the project had been canceled. I countered by maintaining that we had completed all our design effort and then offered to reduce the fee by a small amount—allowed because we had not had to receive tenders and recommend contract award. But the client would not accept the reduced fee, nor would he reveal why he thought the price should be lowered by a greater amount. "Sayed," I finally said to him after four more hours of polite but fruitless discussion, "I must apologize. I can't understand what motivates you. I have justified our fee. Why do you want a lower price?" "It's simple," he replied sheepishly. "The prime minister told me not to pay you one piaster more than 90 percent of the balance now due you." Then he shrugged his shoulders and said, "What can I do?" "If I accept, when can we expect payment?" "Our accountant will hand over the check in about fifteen minutes." A handshaking ceremony ensued, and a great lesson was learned. Both sides were satisfied and a standoff averted. It was a matter of "face" for my client; he could now report success to the prime minister. The reduction in fee was less than the interest that would have been lost if payment were held up another six months.

■ *Know Your Price Limitations.* A rock-bottom or "dropdead" price should be established for every contract negotiation. About the only real commodity a design professional has to sell is the time of his staff. If a negotiated fee does not allow a sufficient professional effort and adequate return on capital invested, the proposal should be withdrawn. Therefore, top management should agree on a minimum price and scope for each international project.

Some firms may occasionally take contracts at a losing price in hopes of gaining a future profitable job from the same client to offset the loss. This logic is invalid. There will always be another firm in the international market foolish enough to make a lower offer than yours, often for an inferior professional job. Avoid this trap by establishing a rock-bottom price before every negotiation.

Know "when to hold and when to fold." Sometimes negotiations deteriorate to such a level that the project loses its professional appeal. This happened, for example, on a project in Africa in which I had worked out with the client the scope of effort and the design fee. We had established design criteria in keeping with the type of project after long consultation with the client. When we delivered the preliminary drawings, the client was pleased, but the financing agency made drastic changes in the quality and type of construction. The agency judged that the project was "too good" for that developing country! This turn of events discouraged us professionally. So we withdrew from the project and, ultimately, were awarded our claim for the effort we had expended up to the time of withdrawal.

There is a time in negotiations when it is best to call a halt and to study airline schedules. In the above case, one of our senior partners announced his decision by saying, "Pack your bag. We're leaving." When scopes of work cannot be reconciled and fee negotiations begin to resemble the process for selling Persian carpets, the dedicated professional will cut losses and look to other markets. It may surprise some that this condition exists almost as much in industrialized countries as in the rapidly developing markets.

■ *Rehearsals and Coaching.* Negotiation rehearsals and coaching are important. Rehearsals work best when a person with the same cultural background as the client plays that role. Local universities can usually supply graduate students or instructors who will welcome the chance to take part in mock negotiations. Extraordinary help is available for coaching professionals to negotiate in the international market. One such organization is Ellen Raider International, Inc., 752 Carroll Street, Brooklyn, New York 11215, and another is Situations Management, Inc., 121 Sandwich Street, Plymouth, Massachusetts 02360. Their combined course "International Negotiations—A Training Program for Corporate Executives and Diplomats" is outstanding. The approach is to teach students to understand the negotiation process and to plan strategies and tactics to use in international negotiations. The cross-cultural and behavioral study program is particularly appealing to professionals who have had some overseas experience. Customized "negotiation rehearsals" are arranged to prepare teams for actual contract discussions. For these, representatives are brought in from the market area culture to play the other side. The training is realistic and valuable to all management levels who may negotiate contracts abroad.

Negotiations for professional services will produce a wide range of results, from simple acceptance to complete rejection. The following dos and don'ts emphasize the principles and main points discussed in this chapter. When followed in practice, they should help ensure your success.

## Dos and Don'ts of Successful Negotiating

- Do take your power of attorney, duly authenticated, to prove your right to represent your firm.
- Don't negotiate when suffering from jet lag. Delay the meeting or arrive at the site a day early, but don't blow the whole deal because your circadian rhythms are upset.
- Do eat before long negotiating sessions. Don't negotiate hungry. Put some chocolate bars, sugar cubes, or a ration of your favorite secret weapon in your briefcase, and use it during the long sessions.
- Don't take too much support material to the meeting. Chances are you won't be able to find what you want when under fire.
- Do have the fee calculations organized on index cards so you can find them and refer to them unobtrusively.
- Don't lose your cool. Remain poised and unflappable. Treat your "adversaries" like future clients.
- Do carefully record all additions and changes which are agreed upon. Stop the meeting, if necessary, to get the record straight.
- Don't fail to have a rock-bottom price.
- Do know when to snap the locks on your attaché case and withdraw gracefully.

# CHAPTER 13

# PROJECT ORGANIZATION AND THE PROJECT MANAGER

The design start date looms over the horizon. The contract has been signed and filed in the home office vault. The manhour estimate has been added to the backlog, and the volume of sales increased by the contract amount.

The international vice president begins to wonder, "Is the project manager nominated in the proposal the right person for the job, and if so, when will he be available?" Telex messages are coming in from the client and the foreign associate. . . . How should an international project be managed? . . . Why should the management approach differ from that used on domestic contracts? . . . Why not throw the foreign contracts in the hopper with those of the county highway department, the local college, and the power company?

To set the scene for discussing the choice of a management system, and for offering guidance, the following basic decisions must be made.

**Basic Decisions**

- Where the design will be performed
- The existing management structure of the design office

- The role of the associate
- The need to be near the client and the project site

**Design Location.**   The days of doing the entire design back at the home office are over. The growth of the design professions in developing countries, the increasing importance of associates, and improved communications have helped force the design location to shift to the project country. But a more compelling force in this shift is that the competition generally is not reluctant to establish design offices in a hostile environment, if that is required to get the contract. For our project we assume that a major portion of the design will be performed in the client's country.

**Management Structure.**   Large design offices, those with a hundred or more employees, have three or four basic management structures:

1. Arrangement by design discipline
2. Arrangement by industry or project type
3. Arrangement by team
4. Single-purpose design offices

*Design Discipline Concept.*   Offices operating on a design discipline concept generally follow a military line and staff system, with a rigid chain of command. Departments are structured as independent design units, such as Civil, Electrical, Mechanical, Structural, Architectural, Geotechnical, Interior Design, Estimating, Specifications, and the like. Support functions such as printing, word processing, translating, personnel, and accounting might be grouped under one administrative manager.

Such an organization, to function efficiently, must have a project management organization superimposed on it. Departments might have from one to fifty separate contracts under design at any one time, each of which is coordinated by one of a group of project managers who have status equal to the department head. The project manager in the organization operating on a design discipline concept plays a very important role, to be discussed later.

*Industry- or Project-Type Concept.*   Offices operating on an industry- or project-type concept place in one department all the disciplines required to perform the design for one industry. Examples are paper mills, highways and railroads, food processing, schools and universities, or hydroelectric power. Huge volumes of contracts are required to fuel such organizations, and, as a result, this type of structure is confined to the largest architectural and engineering firms. The departments tend to become so large that the leader tends to hold vice president status. Very often the departments could be likened to a free-standing architect-engineer operation. Again, a project manager system will be superimposed over the department structure to coordinate projects and to provide a central contact point for the client and for management.

*Team Concept.* Project management by team concept is favored by architects, interior designers, and planners. *Architecture by Team*, by William Wayne Caudill, enthusiastically describes this concept, which works exceptionally well during the planning and preliminary design stages of a contract. Each team is furnished all the design professionals it requires to perform the services described in the scope of work. Outside consultants and specialists can be easily added to the team when needed for short periods of time.

The team concept is a great morale builder, because tasks become less defined and everyone theoretically pitches in where needed regardless of discipline or position. The team works in a physically separate location from the rest of the organization for ease of communication and coordination. There are some negative aspects, which may involve the creation of an elite group, difficulties with quality control, maximum use of company resources, and client relations. Overall, however, a project manager system will be very helpful, and the team leader may double in that role.

*Single-Purpose Concept.* Frequently an engineering project will be so large and of such long duration that it can support a separate design office. Such an operation might be organized on any of the preceding three concepts. Single-client offices tend to be low overhead, no-frills operations, with few such distractions as marketing and proposal preparation. The office manager, or the deputy, will often double in the project manager role.

In discussions of project management that follow, one of the preceding operating concepts will be assumed.

**The Associate's Role.**   The associate has collaborated during proposal preparation, interviews, presentations, and negotiations and may become a full professional partner.

Suppose that a major portion of the design effort, ranging from 20 to 50 percent of the contract, will be accomplished in the host country—this may be a requirement of the contract. If the associate has a well-organized design office capable of producing high-quality professional work, organizing for the contract may be relatively simple. By stationing a senior project manager, a chief engineer or a chief architect, and a few senior designers in the office, the associate's production may be enhanced and the quality of his professional work assured. A very satisfying joint relationship could result. However, if the associate has a weak staff, more professionals from the home office or new recruits may be needed. It will probably take a design chief and a project manager type to bring the associate's office to a production and quality level that will deliver acceptable contract documents.

**The Project Manager—Key to Client Liaison.**   No matter how well your associate knows the client, there is an implicit need to have a company officer at hand to deal with client relations on almost a daily basis. If your man on the scene is developing well and getting along with the associate and the client, that is the natural person for the job. After all, that's really what the person was hired for, and you already have invested a year's funding in him. Reinforce your man on the scene and clarify his relations with the associate, so that together they will maintain a good professional and commercial liaison with the client for the life of the contract.

All the preceding discussions about organizational concepts have emphasized the project manager role. Regardless of the form your organization takes, there must be one person who relates to the client and who can commit the firm to the timely completion of its obligations. In an earlier era, a senior partner could carry out this role, traveling by ship and train and communicating by mail and cables. But now there is a need for rapid reaction, face-to-face consultation, and professional presence which cannot be satisfied in any way other than by a project manager—or perhaps even a partner or a vice president.

The project manager system has been criticized as one which imposes another layer of executives requiring secretaries, automobiles, travel expenses, and lots of perquisites. In my opinion, there is no other acceptable means of handling the coordination and client relations required by a large foreign design or construction management contract. A competent international manager, working full time on projects—and there is no other way—will be invaluable and will release senior partners from these related duties for more meaningful and less tedious tasks.

The role of the international project manager (PM) is not for anyone averse to variety and change. All the miscellaneous tasks which the PM would not assign to a senior professional for fear that they would be considered demeaning seem to end up in the PM's lap. A PM must be able to wrap packages, cash checks, translate menus, drive foreign cars, and know the difference between bribery and "grease." Other attributes involve solid professional references, an unblemished reputation, and a love of travel. It also helps if the PM is a "people person" who can organize and direct task forces. If someone qualifying on one-half of these counts becomes a PM, that person deserves to be one of this elite group. To be successful, any design firm in the export market should have a cadre of these peerless professionals.

As soon as the contract is signed, the project manager should be named by the CEO. Some firms use a formal letter appointing the PM, directed to the nominated person but widely circulated to emphasize the appointment. The client should be officially advised by telex, because the PM will be the client's account executive and main point of contact.

*Duties of the Project Manager.*    The first task of the PM is job planning. All the project-related material should be studied, including trip reports and marketing files. The contract and the scope of work should be studied until they are almost committed to memory. In fact, a copy of each of these documents, *excluding financial information*, should always be at hand in the PM's desk and briefcase. The PM should start planning before other personnel are assigned to the project. A week or so should be allowed in order to work out a critical-path chart for the design effort, to split the job with the associate and other offices, and to formulate a staffing chart for the home office part of the design effort.

The PM's next task after initiating job planning is the budget. The priced proposal and the subsequently negotiated contract price are the basis for the budget. However, direct labor costs have to be entered into the cost accounting system so that periodic budget reports will pick up the new contract. Since cost accounting for projects is now routine with domestic firms, no accounting problems are likely.

The budget for the associate's effort can be a challenge, and the PM may have to establish cost accounting procedures for the foreign associate.

The direct cost budget covering expenses for travel and subsistence, consultants, surveyors, soils borings and tests, and similar items should also be established. Since the PM will control and approve the direct expenses, the budget will be a very important tool. No expenditures should be incurred without the PM's knowledge.

The PM should next focus attention on organizing a site visit by the design team's representatives. The scope of work should be given to the design section leaders for study. Each discipline should be asked to provide a professional for the site visit team, plus a complete list of questions and items needed before preliminary design can start. The PM should compile these questions in a set of notebooks for the site visit team, with spaces for the answers to be written after each question. Duplicate questions should be eliminated, and input from the associate should be solicited. The notebook should contain site maps, pertinent excerpts from the scope of work, and any special background that will help the visiting group. The PM should schedule and plan the site visits and coordinate meetings with the client's staff.

Another important function of the PM is to work with the technical department heads to get the design started correctly. Scopes of work range in detail from skimpy to sophisticated. Examples: The scope of work for a 250-bed regional hospital in Libya was little more than a short paragraph; the scope of work for a small job for the U.S. Army Corps of Engineers might include twenty-five pages of details. The PM will guard against starting any design until the concept of the project is fully agreed with the client. Before the site visit, single-line drawings, sketch maps of the site, and long lists of evocative questions should be prepared. A major goal of the trip will be to obtain all the client's requirements. If the design were to proceed without this preliminary clarification and client approval, much time and labor would be wasted and the consultant would have no grounds for claiming additional fees. Many consultants new to international work have foundered by assuming too much at the beginning of design.

The routine duties of the PM will cover a wide range and will vary between organizations. A PM on an international project will have a much larger role than on a domestic one. For instance, the international PM becomes the expert on host country customs, traditions, geography, geology, currency, and weather. Customs regulations, visa requirements, and the need for vehicle operator's licenses and inoculations are typical of the type of information that a PM should have at fingertip reach.

After design starts, the PM's role will become more routine. The main tasks involve communicating with the client for information needed during design. It is the PM who should first detect that the client may be contemplating a design change. At this signal, the job is to get all the details as quickly as possible and to make a judgment as to whether the client wants a *real* design change or whether the request is a normal one contemplated by the scope of work during the conceptual or preliminary design.

Client relations may depend on how these requests are received. The PM must be firm without being negative. If the change involves a significant amount of labor and delay, the client should be advised. The contract provisions for additional compensation and time should be studied and discussed with the client. The client's request might then be withdrawn or it may become the basis for an *extra* claim.

The PM must keep impeccable records of communications with the client and make memos for the record of all telephone conversations and meetings. The PM's job diary may become an important exhibit in billings or claims for extra compensation.

Another routine duty for the PM will be the periodic billing to the client. The accounting department should be led by hand through the requirements, language, and currency of the contract. The PM should arrange for delivery of the invoice in a positive way and enlist the services of the associate as a collection agent because of the latter's vested interest in getting paid.

Even though your man on the scene calls on the client routinely, the PM should plan regular visits during the design period. These trips can coincide with design conferences, presentations, fact-finding missions, and even invoice collection. The client will appreciate the visit if it is scheduled in advance, and it may lead to new work or additions to the contract. The client also deserves to see someone from the home office top management once in a while, for your firm has been entrusted with the most important project in the program. Client visits should be a first priority for the PM, who should continually update the travel schedule accordingly.

In summary, the PM's position should be less than that of the CEO but higher than your representative on the scene and very different from that of the associate. The PM has responsibility for the firm's performance and should be able to defend it, speaking for the firm when dealing with the client, and of this there should be no doubt. If the man on the scene is also a strong character, there may be a need for formal delineation of responsibility and authority.

The PM assigned to the project country has a role which presents different challenges from those of the counterpart in the home office. There can be many reasons for deciding to design the entire job overseas. Certain types of civil work such as highways, irrigation projects, dams, and even airports seem to "travel" well.

The PM's role abroad includes coordination, but its main functions will be consultant, teacher, public relations officer, and "utility" person. If the project is being designed in the local associate's office, there will be much package wrapping and delivery, purchasing of office supplies, specification writing, proofreading, and design. Collateral duties will include building bridges to several cultures and organizing production of the associate's design force to meet quality control and schedule requirements.

In the home office, the PM communicates with professionals and technicians in one language. Overseas, the PM often gives instructions through an interpreter or in his own second language. Then depending on the audience, the person must explain what is wanted, demonstrate how to do it, and perhaps finally complete the job personally. Despite the obvious challenges, project management abroad is a very rewarding experience. A few years as PM for a consultant on a highway design and construction contract or a hydroelectric power project will do wonders for an engineer's patience, language facility, diplomacy, and grasp of engineering fundamentals.

Probably the most demanding project manager assignment is in construction management or supervision at the project site. Projects financed by international lending agencies and, in fact, any multimillion-dollar expenditure by a public agency for infrastructure will require an on-site staff to coordinate engineering, construction, and start-up. Acceptable candidates for these positions will have all the background previously described, plus maturity and hands-on construction experience.

The duties of the assignment begin with complete professional understanding of the design, specifications, and construction contract. The PM's responsibility is broadly that of the owner's representative, and the challenge is to complete a high-quality construction job on time and within budget. This seems quite simple, doesn't it?

The PM must be capable of chairing a meeting at the site with all the involved parties. Imagine Italian consultants, French general contractors, Portuguese penstock installers, Peruvian tunnel builders, Mexican grouting experts, Nicaraguan government representatives, and an American construction manager gathered at the site to discuss extra work or a design change! Four or five languages, two systems of measurement, bad weather, flooded creeks, and lack of cement might be only a few of the problems for the PM in a typical meeting.

Besides on-site duties, the client will need the PM for a political buffer, a sounding board and advocate. When the president of the country comes to the site to lay the cornerstone, who coordinates the program? When the lending institution gets a bit sticky about why the job is behind schedule, the PM may be sent off to Washington to put oil on the water. If the contractor cannot meet the specification requirements for pumpcrete consistency, the PM may have to step into the gap and become a teacher. If the tunnel contractor's people get frivolous in storing and handling explosives, the PM must decide when to intervene.

The success of the consultant's contract depends on the performance of the person selected for the PM role. Of all project manager assignments, the one at the construction site has the most general and demanding requirements.

With such unusual job specifications, where do the candidates for managers of international design and management consultants get educated? Who would want such a job anyway? In times of national emergency, the U.S. Navy recruits professionals as reserve officers, and after a short intensive training period, these "ninety-day wonders" are shipped off to war. But the engineering profession has no similar "quick fix" for project managers.

In spite of increasing emphasis on formal teaching of construction engineering and management, the main source of managerial candidates seems to be from a kind of apprentice-like on-the-job training system. In common with all systems of learning by doing, this is a haphazard and time-wasting experience. When the time for engineering education, with some postgraduate-level management courses, is added to five or more years in design and perhaps another five in construction supervision, the candidates are likely to be approaching forty years of age before their first PM assignment.

Language skills and knowledge of other cultures are desirable; their acquisition requires motivation and learning ability. Family situations become a major factor, along with professional goals. Small wonder that good project managers are hard to find.

A significant attraction for pursuing the PM path is frequently not obvious to design professionals. It is that project management offers professional gratification to those who are attracted toward people-oriented assignments and challenged by an opportunity to see designs translated into operating facilities. Time is required for this desire to develop and these aptitudes to be recognized. A few years in the field, after some solid design experience, may well direct one's career to construction management.

Another fairly obvious result of PM experience is opportunity to advance to higher positions in management and to ultimately win consideration for entrepreneurial roles. Project managers become pragmatic, and their experience shows when they are seated at the table with peers who have come up the ladder through the design or academic route. Stock ownership, partnership, and directors' appointments are prizes open to senior project managers.

A few examples of problems encountered and solved by project managers abroad will illustrate the value of the system:

■ In Libya our specifications for highway construction were regarded as insane. The requirements for compacting embankment and base course with optimum moisture were considered impossible. The contractor's superintendent thought that the quantity of water specified would turn the project into a sea of mud. The determined PM put on a demonstration of the proper way to construct the embankment by setting up a test section 1 kilometer long. Contrary to all traditional construction practice, the PM relieved the contractor of any responsibility for that section of the road and proceeded to give exact "hands-on" instruction to the foreman and operators who constructed the test section. Having been shown how to do it, the contractor continued to follow the PM's example and completed the job successfully.

- Constructing the royal palace in a remote area taxed the ingenuity of our unflappable PM. All utility lines were buried, and the palace grounds were a maze of water, sewer, irrigation, storm drains, and electric and telephone cables. The Italian contractor had a fairly relaxed attitude about the wisdom of all this. The PM converted one wall of his office to a large drawing of all of the underground installations at a scale of 1 to 50. The systems were color-coded, and every place where the piping crossed or came close, a three-dimensional detail was drawn on the wall to show clearances. This simple procedure got the contractor to organize effectively.

- In Nicaragua the concrete aggregate specifications carried a statement that "sufficient quantities of coarse and fine aggregates were available on the site." When it came time to have site visits by prospective bidders, high water had carried the sand away from the river banks. The amount of coarse aggregate available from existing quarries could not meet the project's demands. The PM requisitioned a construction geologist and instituted a search for aggregate by a drilling program. Proven sources of acceptable aggregate thus found in sufficient quantities for the job had a noticeable effect on subsequent bids and saved money for the owner.

- Engineers who can train technicians in foreign countries are the unsung heroes of the consulting profession. Latin America has a legacy from U.S. professionals who have left behind protégés scattered from Mexico to Chile, each well grounded in basic engineering skills. In Ecuador our PM created a highway and bridge design department out of a mixture of expatriate and local professionals, with engineering and architectural students as drafters. All of the consultant's staff served as teachers, advisers, and consultants.

International consulting is made more attractive to professionals who discover the great rewards from teaching and leading others to develop self-sufficiency. This aspect of foreign projects is often overlooked when viewed from the home base. The idea that the expatriates' teaching role will soon provide all the engineering talent needed in many lands is really not valid. We see Mexico, Venezuela, and Colombia where local professionals are very well organized and completely capable of meeting their countries' engineering needs in many sectors. Yet only two years before this book was published, an elder statesman of the profession in Mexico told me, "The needs of Mexico for infrastructure design will not be satisfied by the human resources available." In my opinion, project managers who can lead and teach foreign professionals will always be required.

Management of international projects requires strong leaders, and the PM system is the only practical way to develop them. Project management can be taught, but not before the student knows what engineering and construction are all about. The fundamentals should be learned, the basics mastered, and then a period of on-the-job exposure scheduled. If an engineer is ideally suited for construction management and has a modest amount of the "right stuff," the person will not remain in the "rookie" category very long. The word will get around the network, and opportunities will be presented.

Several attributes are essential for project management candidates:

- *Competence.* The professional who aspires to a project management assignment need not be a world-renowned designer. But the person should be a journeyman engineer in his chosen field with ability to make presentations, explain designs, and to defend his decisions.

- *Priorities.* The individual must have a firm grip on priorities. A project manager cannot wall himself off from staff or client when problems are breaking out on the project.

- *Planning.* An ability to visualize the critical path for design and construction must be developed. What to do when the river is in flood stage, when to order more cement, and when to work overtime should be decided before the crisis.

- *Awareness.* A sense of "what's happening" is critical. A good PM should know as much as possible about the country and the client, as well as about the project.

- *Communications skills.* A knowledge of languages including one's own is an invaluable asset. There may be good project managers who lack language skills, but to the best of my knowledge there are no outstanding examples of inarticulate leaders in the field.

- *Professional curiosity.* A "state-of-the-art" knowledge of equipment, materials, and engineering practice is required. Continued interest in education and developments in the profession must be maintained.

- *Leadership.* The project manager will know when to delegate and when to act alone. The ability to supervise professionals is an essential quality of the successful PM.

- *Respect for other cultures.* Successful international PMs will show respect for other cultures. This attribute should be in evidence before considering any manager as a candidate for an overseas assignment.

This uncommon combination of skills, training, and personal attributes is desirable because the role of international project manager is broader and more demanding than any other management assignment in the design professions. The project manager may need to be a designer, a construction manager, a construction superintendent, a businessperson, and a diplomat. There is no prototype or role model for the position, which is mastered only through on-the-job training, a system that often produces human failure. But the system does work. People-oriented individuals will find a project management career enhancing and professionally rewarding. The inescapable requirement of "paying dues" during formative years holds the promise of recognition and reward for the survivors of an imperfect system.

## CHAPTER 14

# FOREIGN OFFICE MANAGEMENT LOGISTICS

When the professional services contract requires a significant portion of the design to be accomplished with an associate, an overseas production office must be established. If the local associate has excess staff and office space, the logistics become simple. The joint venture could move onto another floor in the same building, with a few senior professionals and a project manager "seconded" from the home office, and the transition to the new contract might go very smoothly. But this devoutly to be wished situation hardly ever occurs.

The local associate usually has no staff or is overloaded with work. Office management is usually lax, quality control neglected. Our premise is that for any significantly complex or sophisticated design contract the joint venture will need a new office in the project country.

In another typical case, the project might be in a hostile environment, where the operation of a design office would be very challenging, such as operating in Oman, El Salvador, Zaire, or Lebanon. Then the design office might be located relatively close to the job site in a country which provides a good labor pool, acceptable living conditions, excellent communications, and a favorable tax climate. Rome, Athens, Bahrain, Panama, Bangkok, and other similar places have all been havens for international design offices at certain periods in recent history.

It is not unusual for American architect-engineers who are serving the Department of Defense to have been encouraged to open permanent offices near the headquarters of contracting officers for military construction and engineering, so that service would be available on design contracts of all sizes. London, Paris, Rome, Frankfurt, Wiesbaden, Madrid, Ankara, Athens, Bangkok, and Saigon all have been popular locations for U.S. architectural and engineering firms engaged in defense projects.

The point is that the location of the foreign office will not be the result of some brilliantly logical feasibility study. Site selection always has been and always will be thrust on the consultant by fate—usually a Hobson's choice, resulting in a location which no one in the home office thought was a terrific idea. It is generally left up to the project manager (PM) to work minor miracles and to get on with the job.

The country thus having been selected by the client, the associate, or by chance—but rarely by the PM—the only choices the latter might have left are the city, the city section, and/or the building where the office will be located. Very often there is not a wide selection. Good communications and convenience to the client and the associate usually govern. In rapidly developing countries, the options often will include only residential apartment space. Either open-plan office buildings have not been built in the present stage of development, or the cost of rental is more than the architect-engineer can afford. Annual rentals of $600 per square meter ($55.80 per square foot) are common. However, if the budget will accommodate open-plan space or a store front, very acceptable architectural and engineering offices can be put together for the big international project. Groups of apartments are so inefficient that the next best alternative to a store front might be the construction of a preengineered building—which always seem to be available in rapidly developing countries.

Location of the overseas office in a city like Athens, Rome, or Frankfurt is relatively easy but not without pitfalls. These cities have real estate agents who rub their hands with glee when they sense the presence of a foreigner in dire need. I once rented a very attractive open-plan office in the heart of Frankfurt's red light district—a fact that did not surface for several months.

In Italy, it is wise to keep one's lawyer handy, to avoid signing a rental contract which may require almost complete reconstruction when it is time to vacate the premises. At the time the keys to the new office space are turned over, there is usually nothing inside except toilet fixtures and electrical wires protruding from the junction boxes. The rest is up to the tenant.

Now is the time to use some of the architectural expertise that the firm is selling to the public. The best approach is to bring in a senior architect from the home office to work with a local designer who knows what is available in the market. Together they can turn out an interior design and a budget. Their challenge will be to provide an atmosphere which will be a credit to the firm's international reputation, yet meet a tight budget using furniture and fixtures available locally. Unfortunately, meeting this challenge will necessitate making compromises among what is wanted, what is affordable, and what is available that will haunt the PM for the rest of his foreign service. But it serves a second useful purpose—it introduces the PM to the international market. It can come as a big surprise to the PM that this trade-off has to be confronted even before the first project design drawing is started!

**Office Layout.** The office layout will be the first stumbling block for the local planning professionals—and maybe to your new associates, if they are involved. The theory of office planning in developing countries, and even in Europe, is as follows:

- Put top management in the corners with the best exposure. Provide them with plush offices, each with two doors—front and back, offering easy escape from any unwelcome visitors—and a formal conference room for board meetings.
- Squeeze the professionals and technicians into the rest of the space, at the rate of about 8 square meters per person. Install them in small offices without windows, using "bullpen" areas for technicians and clerks, with narrow aisles, sparse toilet facilities, no conference rooms, and no exit except through the front door (so the help can't escape!).

The challenge will be to confront this mentality head-on and to lay out an efficient working office for the multinational staff. Some of the features to include in an architectural and engineering office plan are as follows:

1. Adequate but functional offices for top management, with conference facilities for department head meetings, presentations, and use as a "situation" room
2. The location of support functions out of the traffic pattern so accounting, employment, purchasing, the travel department, and similar services will have a secluded and private area
3. Open-plan areas for each discipline or functional department, according to the management structure, provision of conference rooms, library, and central files
4. Printing, photography, word processing, specifications, and estimating areas in a location for easy access by the design staff
5. Realistic planning for storage of supplies
6. Secure and fireproof areas for storage of work in progress
7. Drafting room illumination planned on an area system to eliminate "spot" lighting, intensity conforming to drafting room standards
8. Functional and attractive but not monumental design for entire office, with goal of depreciating most of the expense on a series of long-term contracts, so that the investment does not become a long-term debt

**Equipping the Office.** The senior architect from the home office imported to design the office and make a budget estimate will likely require about ten days on site. The planning can then be completed at the home office.

When contracts for interior decoration, partitions, furniture, and fixtures are awarded, a local professional employee should be assigned the job of resident architect to handle the day-to-day contacts. This person will be more efficient than one from the home office, because of language facility and knowledge of local practice. Running around town to select paint colors and carpet samples is no job for a department head. The imported talent should be hard at work during this period, planning the design effort for the big contract.

There are certain "big ticket" equipment items that must be considered carefully before selection, such as internal telephone systems, telex machines, air conditioning, computers, word processors, duplicating and printing machines, and microfilm equipment. The wise manager determines which machines are available in the market, the level of maintenance offered on them, and the supply of spare parts and consumables on hand at the local dealers. Except in rare cases, it is not prudent to bring in complicated equipment (computers, word processors, or printing machines) not already available and serviced locally.

Selection of furniture and hardware for an international office will pose problems to the international project manager. At home, the office probably was furnished before the PM was hired—and in a fairly traditional manner. But now the task will be to provide workstations for perhaps a hundred professionals and technicians. A market study for drafting tables, stools, reference tables, and desks may reveal that economical or functional furniture is just not available. The best alternative could be to design a simple table, to be covered with coated paper and equipped with a high-quality parallel ruler. Civil engineers need drafting machines, and some European drafters will favor vertical drafting boards. Open-plan, shoulder-height partitions are simple to build and should be considered.

Hardware will present a much more difficult problem. If the home office is fully computerized, with computer-assisted design (CAD) and drafting systems, it would be a rude shock to the PM to learn that the board of directors expects the international office to be equipped with obsolete or elementary equipment. The limit on investment in advanced electronic equipment to be installed in an overseas office will depend on many factors, but the following few will control:

1. Budget
2. Local availability
3. Maintenance and service
4. Power supply reliability and characteristics
5. Trained operators
6. Acceptance by local employees
7. Projected life of contract
8. Budget (first and last)

At the minimum, electric typewriters and word processing equipment will be needed. Since many other languages besides English are apt to be used, the equipment chosen as a standard should be able to handle Spanish, French, English, and the language of the host country. This probably means using typewriters with interchangeable type fonts, such as the IBM Selectric typewriter.

Specification preparation for international projects is a special problem, because many references to such sources as German DINs, British Standards, French Norms, and FIDIC contract documents will be made. Word processors or general computers are needed to store and retrieve specifications. This equipment must be included in the budget and the space requirements from the start. Estimates in themselves may also pose a new problem, because international projects usually require increasingly refined and detailed estimates at each stage of the planning and design. Contracts in countries with British traditions will be based on the quantity survey system, which may impose new formats and regimens on the design staff. Cost data from the field must be stored on tapes or disks. Hardware selection requires compatibility with the home office, the associate's office, and perhaps with the client.

The development of engineering professionals requires microcomputers as standard equipment—as has the tough competition in the international market. Hardware selection needs thoughtful attention before the office budget is finalized. The use of computer bureaus should not be overlooked. IBM, Control Data, Nixdorf, Philips, and others have service bureaus in major cities and provide good options for designers. But my experience with the industry giants suggests that you might want to rely on your own tried-and-true programs or, better yet, have your own staff do all programming.

In planning the office layout, a communications room for telex and facsimile machines should be located in the front section near the PM, whose secretary can then monitor telex traffic. Practically all important communications will come through this route. Because of time differences, many messages will come in during the nonworking hours, and they should be received in a secure place. Tape-recorder answering devices for receiving messages from the home office and your "man on the scene" should be located in the communications room. Supplies of telex paper, a paper shredder, and time zone clocks should also be located here.

Because the overseas office is being established to fill a pressing need—producing contract documents for a new contract—staff should be "breathing down the necks" of the painters and telephone installers. This tactic is to get planning and early production items, such as the site investigation report, underway without delay. To expedite the beneficial occupancy date of the new office, the PM should have the staff busy with some operating tasks. For example, a design office will use a large amount of paper and pencils—office supplies of a predictable nature. A request for price quotations should be sent out to a short list of reputable office supply firms, and an open-end contract entered into, which provides for fast delivery service. The contract should be renewable on a short-term basis until the supplier establishes a good track record.

Contracts for telex installation, printing, typewriter repair, and duplicating should be handled in the same manner. The budget for these items will be considerable, so during the early stages the PM and the staff should conclude agreements for all essential services.

At the same time, a driver-messenger should be considered a necessary staff member. In major cities, the PM should not do the driving on daily business missions. Perhaps in smaller countries the matter is not of importance, but in developing countries, having a driver is a matter of status. It makes great sense, too, where the driver can deliver important messages, make bank and post office runs, and meet visitors at the airport. Time saved in car maintenance, parking, delivering packages, and chauffeuring visitors will soon prove the wisdom of this appointment. In one large foreign office a staff of three drivers also operated printing and duplicating machines and performed minor custodial chores very efficiently.

Housekeeping for a large design office should be handled by contract cleaners after working hours. Since the client's staff will be in the overseas office regularly—perhaps even permanently—and simply as a matter of good business practice, good order and cleanliness are important. Housekeeping staff should not be in the office during business hours—the professional atmosphere should be carefully maintained.

The scope of work should be studied during the early days to identify special services that will be needed later on and to check their availability. Printers, artists, model makers, and photographers should be visited and interviewed, their references checked for the services anticipated. Much disappointment and aggravation can be avoided by selecting these people early. If certain scale models and architectural renderings will be required for preliminary presentations, good creative people should be selected and the production period reserved in a preliminary way in their schedules.

International consulting means travel in big quantities. One of the best tranquilizers for a busy PM is a capable travel agency. Since its services are included in the price of the tickets, there is no real expenditure. Your business is appreciated, because two or three consulting firms will provide volume for a solid base to any small agency. One person in the design office should be assigned as the authorized liaison, so the agent will not have to deal with individuals. Visas, hotel reservations, ground transportation, and car rentals can all be handled by this agency, which will deliver tickets by messenger. Using a travel agent is an excellent way of controlling travel policies for the category of hotels assigned to various grades of employees, as well as the class of air travel. Travel agent's bills for air fares can be paid by air travel cards, so credit is facilitated.

The options described above which the architect-engineer project manager may choose in establishing a production office do not cover an all-inclusive list of such problems. I seek to present the planning of an overseas production office in a positive manner which will stimulate original thinking.

Almost any labor-saving device or system accepted and used at home can probably be adapted to use by professionals and technicians in your overseas office. But local culture and tradition must be considered before trying to force what might be space age technology down the throats of a very proud and capable staff. A typical example will illustrate the point.

When I went to Italy in 1963 as manager of the European operations of a U.S. architectural and engineering firm, the organization was using tracing paper, india ink, and a great variety of template systems for lettering. My first reaction was to get rid of the paper, ink, pens, and lettering templates and to legislate the use of Mylar drafting sheets, plastic pencils, stick-on lettering systems, press-on type, and even adhesive sheets for crosshatching, shading, and symbols. It seemed that I had been relegated to the green eyeshade era, almost unknowingly. Fortunately, I had come to Europe after some years in a more primitive environment and realized the traumatic shock of sudden change. Together with our senior multinational professionals—Italian, French, German, British, Arab, and others—we instituted a pilot program. A small amount of supplies were imported from Germany, England, and the United States. Three or four of our finest Italian designers were selected for the "experiment," and they were trained, in-house, to use the new materials. Very shortly they became proficient and even innovative. In turn, they were established as instructors. After a very short time, paper and linen sheets, lettering templates, pens, and ink were all but extinct. The change was so dramatic that one day there was a great panic when no ink could be found in the office for the chief architect to use in signing the title blocks of an important design!

One of the major objections to the use of Mylar sheets was the cost. In an Italian design office, one never thinks of labor as a cost until payday. But direct expense for supplies, travel, rent, and the like was always the subject of prolonged and heated discussions. However, paper sheets with drawings in ink could not be salvaged, so when there was a design change the uncompleted sheet would be abandoned and placed in the project plan file. To attempt to control changes and labor costs, a careful review was made of the uncompleted sheets at the conclusion of each project. An estimate was made of the lost manhours, and if the sheet was abandoned because of a change in scope of work, an attempt would be made to recoup from the client some of the costs. Unfortunately, the bulk of the spoiled drafting sheets resulted from errors or design changes generated by our own staff.

A year or so later, I decided to examine the plan files of a particularly troubled project and to study the incomplete tracings. The job captain said, "But we don't have any wasted sheets. When we make a change, we just erase the pencil. If it's a big area, we wash off the pencil with a wet cloth. We make duplicate originals of incomplete sheets to show the work expended before a change has been ordered." The use of Mylar sheets cut down on the number of wasted sheets, the drawings were of routine high quality, and drafting time was appreciably reduced by the switch to pencil drafting.

**Records.**   Some architectural and engineering offices look like museum file rooms. Rolls of prints in all stages of deterioration litter the premises. To avoid this cumbersome filing system and improve office appearance, microfilm all record drawings. Use the aperture card system and negotiate a bulk microfilm contract with a laboratory. Microfilming can be done at off-peak times, in large batches. Files and microfilm readers should be placed in strategic locations in the design office. When it becomes necessary to reproduce a full-sized scale drawing from the film, the laboratory should be able to provide copies in a reasonable turnaround time.

Every office should have an ongoing records disposal program. It is of no value to microfilm irrelevant correspondence, design sketches, and voided estimates. A good method for handling the decision of deciding what will be microfilmed is to appoint a small committee of senior professionals who will make a microfilming schedule and update it every three months or so.

Change comes slowly in international offices, and not without bruised pride and egos. On reflection, this condition should not be new to project managers who have worked for long-established U.S. engineering firms. Younger professionals all around the world are receptive to new production methods, and they should be used as leaders when changes are necessary. Discussions of logistics eventually lead to a study of the personnel management of professionals, particularly multinationals. The next chapter will be a sounding board for some concepts in this area. But first, here is a short list of dos and don'ts relating to logistics.

## Dos and Don'ts of Logistics

- Do use your own professionals to design the new office.
- Do assign the responsibility for supervising the installation to a local professional.
- Do consider local customs and traditions before introducing startling changes.
- Do select hardware after a study of available service facilities.
- Do plan a "world-class" functional and attractive workplace which can be proudly displayed to prospective clients.
- Don't build monumental overseas offices.
- Don't overlook microcomputers and computer bureaus.
- Don't disregard the services of a travel agent.

# CHAPTER 15

# THE FOREIGN OFFICE— MANAGING MULTINATIONALS

A foreign design office is invariably multinational. It is increasingly difficult to get senior American professionals to serve overseas for long periods. If local professionals are available, it makes sense to employ them, because they and their families do not have to be moved or supported. If the contract requires two languages, it increases the need for local nationals. Finally, foreign spouses or family of local citizens have preferred status for obtaining work permits. In the larger cities of the world, U.K. and U.S. citizens married to locals are an excellent source of professional, secretarial, and technical skills. And in the Middle East, Moslem professionals from all over the world have gravitated to share in the construction boom. As a result of these conditions, international architectural and engineering offices tend to have a multinational staff.

To add to this interesting mix, various professions share the same workplace, each with its own traditions, approach to creativity, and jargon. Thirty years of working with architects, engineers, and planners led me to conclude that the trainer who enters the cage with lions and tigers has a task only slightly more sensitive than the PM for an international architectural and engineering organization. My rationalization of this critical situation is that the architect creates graphically, whereas the engineer seeks expression in numbers. To an engineer, $x$'s and $y$'s define a curve, whereas an architect wants to see the line on paper, to draw many variations, and to find a form that is artistically pleasing. Thought processes of the two disciplines are fundamentally poles apart. The architect is concerned with the appearance of the building and its function. The engineer is concerned with the foundation, the structure, the source of power and water, and waste water disposal. The planner will be concerned about the building's ability to meet the needs of its users fifty years ahead.

Merely cracking a whip at these multinational, diverse, and intelligent professionals, as the animal trainer might, doesn't always get their attention. So the management of a multinational mixture of professionals of varying cultures is an interesting challenge offering potentially great rewards. And when the whole team is devoted to the planning and design of a project for a client with yet another culture, management skills may be taxed. One person, no matter how great a possessor of worldly knowledge, will not be able to sense how each of these different people will approach a new design problem. Did the engineer study at Politecnico de Torino? The architect graduated from the University of New Delhi, and the planner got a master's at Columbia. How can we be sure that we are all talking about the same thing? The problem is not inches and centimeters. The areas for lack of understanding are enormous—culture, environment, and education each play a part.

One way to eliminate these gaps is to have working sessions early in the preliminary design stage to study the scope of work and the concept. The establishment of design criteria in a very formal way is about the only means of avoiding confusion. Following this, a detailed basis of design must be prepared, so that it can be understood and checked independently. The planners and architects must describe the reasons for design features in their section of the report. This document should be protected very carefully, and if the client does not require basis of design or a formal design analysis, it should become part of the firm's record documents.

The project manager will have different methods of communicating, some of which may work in one situation but none in every case. For example, I found that large conferences are not of much use in managing complex design jobs. Neither are "memos to the troops" effective. The best system has been "management by walking around," described in *In Search of Excellence*, by Thomas J. Peters and Robert H. Waterman, Jr. The concept is not new to engineers and contractors who have been trained in the field. There is no better (and perhaps no other) way to learn what is happening and to give instructions than a face-to-face meeting on the job site. The resident engineer for a highway project rides over the route daily, in the role of management by walking around. In fact, my lasting impression as a boy visiting a construction job was the sight of the superintendent on horseback directing his foremen. Taking management to the workplace puts the right emphasis on contact with individuals. When the product comes from a person's mind, as in the design professions, management gets very personal. Concepts and design ideas are best dealt with by small-group interaction, and "walking around" is an effective way to manage design groups.

Conferences are necessary for design coordination and for alerting staff to sudden changes in scope or criteria. It is well to limit conferences to four-alarm emergencies and to make the agenda very specific. The list of conferees should be fewer rather than more of those who seem to be essential participants. Almost anything that has to be said to a group of high-paid department heads can be handled in thirty minutes. If there is any doubt, calculate the cost of the meeting at the rates charged clients for professional time including overhead and profit. A conference need not be long and cost several thousand dollars: Was this one really necessary?

Recognizing cultural differences will be a governing factor in structuring internal communications. The practice of management by walking around will overcome most culturally oriented fears, such as loss of face and public embarrassment. Another management principle which has stood the test of time is very aptly stated—"Catch him doing something right, and reward him for it," as expressed in *The One Minute Manager*, by Kenneth H. Blanchard. Awarding kudos is an excellent management style and should be practiced. Professional excellence is an ever-present goal, so fundamental errors have to be corrected. By the time a professional attains enough experience to be included on an international architectural and engineering staff, the person is usually well rounded and competent and is rarely guilty of a lapse. Seasoned professionals enjoy praise too. Professional recognition is often more appreciated than small salary increases.

As project manager on a large highway design contract, I

noticed that the senior partners of the five-hundred-person firm hardly ever visited my area and rarely spoke to junior employees. Management seemed to look on employees only as warm bodies. Making a firm resolution, I asked one of the senior partners to walk with me around my forty-person section every week. By introducing each employee to the "big bosses," I tried to develop some personal contact. The effort worked very well. My team liked the idea. It was the first time many of them had ever been recognized by a partner. Their reactions impressed me greatly and, after that, walks around the office became a habit.

Closely related to face-to-face management is the "open door." In America, much lip service is given to the idea of top management operating with an open-door policy. Even our presidents accept questions from reporters while hurrying to appointments. Other cultures are more reserved. Foreign professionals will not be accustomed to interrupting the president of the company in the corridors, let alone in *his* office. Most company management in Europe or the Middle East works behind several closed doors.

In an international architectural and engineering operation, a manager can signal approachability by touring the office alone, not with other staff, on a random schedule. When in town, which may be only half of the working days, the manager finds it relaxing to get out from behind a desk and to talk with people about all sorts of personal problems which may be perplexing them. The open door should be scheduled so as not to conflict with conferences, telephone calls, and "skull sessions." And when the staff learns that the door can be opened very easily by prior appointment, and your secretary has been instructed that you are available regularly, the respect of local employees is well on the way to becoming established.

Since management and senior professionals will be in travel status frequently, if not continually, it is essential that continuity of leadership be maintained. The organization structure should automatically provide for continuing authority and responsibility when a key person is out of town. Travel schedules should be maintained in each department, and the PM's secretary should be the clearing house for schedules.

More important, there should be a senior person, preferably a company officer or partner, who is deputy to the head of the office. The deputy's role should be clearly established, so the person chosen will be in the office when the leader is away, as well as most of the time when the leader is in town. The deputy should have all the legal powers to act on any matter and should assume command automatically. Employees and clients should be made aware of this situation so that the operation goes on smoothly, unquestioned.

International design offices sometimes collide head-on with local customs. Working hours, coffee breaks, prayer time, and holiday schedules are among the chief sources of conflict if management is insensitive to customs. "Nine to five" is strictly a metropolitan U.S. schedule. In the tropics, office hours tend to start early, when the day is cool, and lunch periods may last two hours. In Athens, office employees tend to go home for the noon meal and perhaps take a siesta, getting back to the office at about 5 P.M., for another two or three hours of work. The big "rush hour" there comes late in the evening. Indeed, in most Latin cities, there are not enough facilities for workers to get lunch downtown, because of the custom of going home for lunch. Cost has something to do with the custom. Middle- and upper-management types may eat in restaurants, but the drafters and secretaries either bring lunch or go home.

In Italy, breakfasts are skimpy. Even the Italian army starts the day off with just an "espresso." By midmorning everyone is hungry. I learned this custom the hard way. During my early days in Rome, I was making an inspection trip to the Livorno office. As I approached the building at about 11 A.M., I noticed some of our employees sitting in a sidewalk cafe. A coffee break was normal enough, but I found the entire office deserted. Not one of the twenty-five employees was at a desk. The switchboard was flashing, phones were ringing, and the vacant office reminded me of a fire drill. Sensing culture shock, I joined the force on the sidewalk. Slowly I realized that the "coffee break" was a time-honored custom and no one wanted to be left out. After a week or so, I convened a few senior Italians to discuss the culture gap on this problem. We came to a happy solution by awarding a concession to one of the snack bars, which sent a waiter to the office every morning and afternoon to push a trolley (company furnished) around the floor to sell the traditional fare.

In Moslem countries, everything stops when one of the five daily calls to prayer comes during the work schedule. Offices generally have an area for group prayer, and this facility is an essential part of the floor plan. The custom was made clear to me when I was in a long line at the Saudia Airline office in

Riyadh hoping to get a space on a flight home. At prayer time the entire staff and some of the clients withdrew from sight. Non-Moslems sat unobtrusively, to wait for prayers to finish— perhaps fifteen minutes.

Unknown traditions can present culture shock. In Panama, when a public figure dies, there is a day of national mourning. Local custom dictates that burial follow within twenty-four hours of death, so the day of mourning arrives with scarcely any notice. Posters with wide black borders appear overnight announcing the event. All offices close for the day. The tradition must be observed by international firms, a rule they often learn by surprise.

Holidays, too, are sometimes difficult to fathom. Carnival week precedes Lent, and the seriousness of the gaiety is often misunderstood by visitors. Attendance at work begins to dwindle for days before Mardi Gras and will probably not get back to normal for some time after. There is no real way to plan production during carnival, so the best advice is "if you can't lick them—join them."

If customs and traditions seem to divert attention from the main purpose of a foreign operation, take heart. The design professions are treated with great respect abroad. Professionals dress and act quite formally in most countries and will appreciate working in an atmosphere that mirrors respect for the professional. On one of my walks around our Rome office, I noticed a British quantity surveyor who had shed socks and shoes and was working blissfully barefoot, oblivious to the world. I, however, was expecting an imminent visit by an inspection team from a potential client and was trying to get the office in condition to reflect an image of professionalism. Taking the man's supervisor aside, I said, "Tell that bloke to get his shoes on—I'm expecting company!" In a few minutes the quantity surveyor appeared in my doorway—fully dressed—socks, shoes, jacket, and tie. "Am I fired?" he asked. When I told him I only wanted him to reflect our serious image for the upcoming visit, he heaved a huge sigh. Managing multinationals takes some understanding.

Labor laws will have as much effect on foreign operations as tradition and custom. Shift and overtime work is not as common abroad as in the United States. Night work requires premium pay. It is illegal to work on Sundays or holidays in many countries, and, of course, in the Arab world, Thursday and Friday are not workdays. With tight delivery schedules for contract documents, the work schedule has to be planned with respect to these factors. To have good employee relations, international architectural and engineering firms need to investigate the labor laws with local legal advisers and accountants. Of course, if overtime, night work, and holiday schedules are required, the premium must be considered and the effort might not be worth the higher cost. Perhaps temporary staff would be a better solution than overtime for workload peaks.

Annual leave and sick leave take on new meaning in international projects. European and Latin staff generally are accustomed to long vacations at regular intervals. Our German secretary, who was a workaholic, planned her month-long vacations several years in advance. This very capable and loyal employee let nothing stand in the way of her rigid leave schedule, since she had her airline tickets and hotel bookings half a year ahead. Such planning is common in many countries. Those of us raised with the Yankee work ethic, which says, "Take your vacation when business permits," adjust poorly to reality. The best solution, it seems, is to make a leave schedule for all departments and adhere as closely as possible to it. This respect for other customs will pay enormous dividends in loyalty and morale.

If annual leave is hard to cope with, consider the impact of sick leave. In countries with a socialized medicine system, sick leave is looked on as an adjunct to annual leave. An employee who may have a minor problem, or none at all, can get written "permission" from a government health officer to "take the baths," or "two weeks in the mountains," which is charged to sick leave. There is not much that an employer can do about this. Payroll overheads often will include a huge percentage for national health insurance. Sick leaves are an additional part of the cost.

In some countries, war veterans have very special privileges. Each Italian employer is supposed to have a certain percentage of war veterans on the payroll. Generally, those seeking placement are unskilled, and since architectural and engineering firms do not have much need for common labor, the problem is minor.

Since international or foreign firms do not have any real status in host countries, labor courts always find the foreigner at fault. An international manager must approach labor problems with extreme caution and excellent legal support.

In supervising professional and technical employees, a program of performance ratings is a valuable management tool. It is sometimes not easy to get the cooperation of senior engineers and architects to rate other professional employees, because they regard the chore as irksome and a bureaucratic nuisance. However, an engineer may be in the wrong assignment or have been employed in a job which is beyond that person's ability, either in terms of the necessary technical knowledge or managerial ability. This is as much a fault of the employer as it is of the employee, and a performance rating system will bring the problem to management attention. The situation may then be remedied by transfer, outplacement, retraining, or reassignment. Rarely is termination required, except in cases of outright incompetence or misrepresentation of professional education and experience.

Employee performance is the key to maintaining effective quality control in a consulting organization. Quality control is complex and worthy of exhaustive treatment. My aim in this book is to call attention to those aspects of a quality control program where international practice is likely to differ from a domestic operation.

Every design firm has had quality control problems. The possibility of design deficiencies, just plain mistakes, and carelessness haunts managers of professionals. Many firms pay great lip service to programs designed to instill quality control principles in their staff. Sometimes the results are not as good as the public relations fodder that is generated. Top management frequently thinks that the product is better than it actually is, because it believes its own propaganda.

Short schedules and fee competition are enemies of quality. The best quality control comes from careful checking at the preliminary design stage. Such checking requires time and money, and much management attention is required to maintain a successful checking operation in international practice. The use of microcomputers and a system of design review by peers eliminates many possibilities of error.

Professionals from other cultures may not adopt quality control procedures as gracefully as one might wish. There is a general tendency for professionals abroad to accept any product of an associate as valid. Then, when differences are found, there is a great beating of chests, accusations, and anger. About the only way to exercise quality control under these conditions is to organize a team effort: Have critical areas examined by two different professionals. Quality control should always be on the agenda, even if certain checking procedures must be carried out after the design is released for bidding.

A manager should be able to detect a tendency on the part of the staff to shift the burden of quality control to the client. There are cases where consulting engineer firms have turned out hurried designs, hoping that errors would be picked up in review by the client. This is a very delicate problem, because some review agencies have a tendency to tear a design to shreds, to defend their national pride. Others, particularly those with a large staff of reviewers who feel that money is being wasted on foreign consultants, delight in finding errors in foundation analysis, surveying, and design criteria. The best defense against all these possibilities is a good "offense," which includes careful checking at every level. Failures in quality control in America usually mean a lawsuit. Failures in quality control abroad mean a canceled contract, a lost client, and a bad reputation. A major factor in international success will be a management attitude of continuous quality control, coupled with support for the design and a willingness to correct design deficiencies when discovered, in a timely manner and without cost to the client.

Management of an international design office with a multinational staff is a demanding responsibility. Morale of such a team as described in this chapter will be an important factor shaping its professional and financial success. Frequently, morale is the key to meeting production schedules and design challenges. To help staff get settled in the new country, the office can provide personal support in many ways: having rental contracts for employees reviewed by the company lawyer; offering support to employees' families while the breadwinners are out of town; and supporting company athletic teams, tennis tournaments, and picnics. Local employees enjoy meeting their associates' families, and the mixing of cultures breaks down some interpersonal barriers that may have developed in the office.

Managing multinationals is not an easy task. A consultant who establishes a design office abroad will select management for that office with great care. Someone who was a great success in a branch office operation in the midwest may be a colossal failure when the umbilical cord to headquarters is cut. The challenges of managing a multinational professional operation are fascinating and rewarding. The following management guidelines are suggested:

- Mixing professions and cultures will produce clashes requiring patience and understanding.
- Opening lines of communication bridges gaps and promotes morale.
- "Management by walking around" is a tried and effective method of managing professionals.
- Eliminate unnecessary conferences and keep the guest list lean.
- Set work breaks, holidays, and working schedules with due regard to customs.
- Consult legal and accounting advisers in all matters concerning labor laws, salaries, and wages.
- Institute a performance rating system.
- Constantly monitor quality control procedures. Don't use the client's staff to check your designs.
- Support expatriate employees in their efforts to get settled in a new country.
- Encourage company-sponsored activities as morale boosters.
- When a professional employee turns in a poor performance, management should know the reason, because usually the employer shares some of the blame.
- Before terminating a senior employee, consider such alternatives as a change of assignment, transfer, or out-placement.

# CHAPTER 16

# MANAGING FOREIGN OFFICE FINANCES

Managing finances for a foreign office is a different cup of tea from supervising logistics and personnel, which might be handled by reaction during the learning period. A new international manager with a few good contracts and some good fortune might muddle through serious logistics and personnel crises and still come out with a profit. Lack of financial planning, however, could put the foreign operation in a vulnerable condition before the cash starts to flow from work in progress. Sound financial planning and management are vital for survival during the first years of a foreign operation.

Architects and engineers as a class—and the best project managers among them—are not noted for being apt financial managers. Usually nothing in their academic or professional training contributes to producing pragmatic cash managers or financial planners. So it is indispensable that before foreign assignment a PM be given a short intensive course in the home office financial system. Such exposure may not be the most satisfying experience in a new manager's career, because of a corporate secrecy policy. Usually, the financial management and strategy of a midsized professional firm is tightly shared between the CEO, the company treasurer, the head of the accounting department, and one of the partners of the accounting firm which audits the books and provides consulting advice. This group sees little benefit from sharing company secrets with a newly appointed foreign manager. The typical chief accountant of an architectural and engineering firm will more likely regard anything away from home shores as deep trouble and almost certain disaster. A short course is a must, however, for both the new foreign office manager and the home office accounting department.

If the foreign operation is new, the manager has a good opportunity to organize a reporting system that will keep him aware of his office's financial condition and also fill the needs of the home office for timely reports. Consulting help from international accounting and law firms with branches in the project country is a first priority. Accounts must be set up to provide the home office with the information it requires and to include all the legal requirements of the local government, for example, accounts for gain or loss due to currency exchange; reserves for mandatory Christmas and Easter bonuses; and liquidation pay, which will be new to the home office and must be explained. There are many other differences in accounting procedures that will baffle the home office accountants.

In addition to fiscal accounting, a cost accounting system must be instituted during the first month of operation. Staff must be trained in accurate timekeeping and allocation of labor and direct costs to specific projects. The basic document is the *time sheet,* which seems to be unknown to professionals of developing countries. Even U.K. and European architects and engineers adapt slowly to formal accounting of hours spent on any specific task. Assigning a contract number to a project and getting completed time sheets required persistent attention in our Rome office. Final resort to a cruel but practical policy— "no time sheet, no paycheck"—resolved the problem, but not without great discussion.

If the home office cost accounting system is considered too cumbersome for a foreign branch operation, there are now a number of alternates for designing your own program. Package software systems are readily available. The National Society of Professional Engineers and the American Institute of Architects have collaborated to develop computer-based financial management systems exclusively for architectural and engineering firms. These tailored programs reduce the need for custom-made software and report forms and are available from

Harper and Shuman, Inc., 68 Moulton St., Cambridge, Massachusetts 02138. Restraints on computer systems abroad, as previously mentioned, include service availability for hardware and a reliable power source.

A key control report will concern progress on each contract in hand. It is the manager's most important tool. Since it cannot be completed until accounting reports are finished, the need for having monthly figures on hand a few days after the close of the accounting period is obvious. The contract status report reveals which contracts are exceeding budget, the value of the completed work, and the amount of unbilled work. If the management has not detected trouble, this report will signal a need for attention. If labor costs rise and percent completion remains static, management intervention is needed.

Evaluation of work in progress is often difficult in consulting engineering, as is establishing fees for large contracts or terminating senior professionals. Progress is often impeded by lack of field information, design changes, and wrong assumptions during design. When a project manager or department head tries to learn the value of design completed to date in a specific area, such as the air-conditioning system for an office building, the person often draws a blank. Depending on the section manager involved, the answer may run from "almost complete" to "I don't know."

The most common reporting fault in a small firm is the lack of a system to calculate percentage of completion of design. If there are only two or three drawings, an experienced designer might estimate the number of manhours required to finish by studying each sheet. In a project with several hundred design drawings, there must be a system, such as using the design budget and the number of hours already expended. If the design budget is kept up to date to include changes, this method will work. In estimating the completion percentage, the technical department head compares manhours spent to total budgeted for the item in question and reports the percentage to management. The results should be examined with care because if there are basic errors in the original manhour estimate, the job may show 100 percent of the budget expended when there is still work to be done. Many professional firms have gone out of business because of lack of attention to proper evaluation of work in progress.

Progress plotted for design and construction projects follows an S-shaped curve. Advancement is slow during the first weeks, picks up speed during the middle 70 percent, and slows down when nearing completion. Troubled projects show completion in the high 90 percent area for long periods while costs keep mounting. This is due to poor reporting, incompetency, or willful false information. Alert management will carefully investigate "stalled" contracts and take action to get them moving before it is too late to avoid a loss.

General and administrative costs must also be allocated to specific projects. While *general and administrative* overhead is easily defined, it is not very well understood by professionals. Any direct charge which cannot be allocated to a specific project is an overhead cost, which must be charged to all contracts prorated according to the value of each contract in a given period. General overhead charges for overseas operations include heavy travel costs for marketing and supervisory travel by management because of the large area of operations.

*Salary-related overhead* is easy to identify and is generally constant for a long period. It is important to understand both of these overhead items—general and administrative overhead and salary-related overhead—and to be able to explain them to prospective clients in a convincing manner. If a client is not accustomed to dealing with engineering and architectural firms, the prospect of paying fees that are a 2 to 3 multiplier on base labor costs is mind-boggling. Fortunately, the multinational companies generally engage consulting architects and engineers on a cost-reimbursable basis, and their staff is used to dealing with fees in the above range.

In addition to the progress reporting system, proper management will require the following monthly reports: balance sheet and income statement; cash flow; workload projection (uncompleted contracts); accounts receivable; and accounts payable.

- *Balance Sheet and Income Statement.* A balance sheet and income statement (of profit and loss) should be available for management within ten days of the close of the accounting period. The engineering and architectural business has many short contracts and the overseas business cycle may have abrupt changes, so it is very helpful to receive the balance sheet and income statement monthly.

- *Cash Flow.* This report is a valuable tool because it immediately signals the need to collect fees, draw on credit, invest excess cash, or transfer funds to the home office.

- **Workload.** This report comes from the contract status report and job manhour estimates. It is a guide for shifting technical personnel among departments, planning additions to staff, or increasing marketing efforts.

- **Accounts Receivable.** Professionals are notoriously allergic to collecting fees, and the monthly review of accounts over thirty, sixty, and ninety days past due may indicate that the PM or the senior partner must take immediate action to expedite collections.

- **Accounts Payable.** This report is a check on good business practice by the staff. The prompt payment of normal accounts makes a good image for an international firm and deserves the attention of top management.

There is one other report which is a simple summary of progress or lack of it—a graphic showing the sales goal and the operating costs goal. The actual accumulated figures are plotted each month, and thus the profit figure for the year to date is expressed clearly. This is a good chart to prepare for visitors from the home office. It is disarmingly simple, but very useful.

The above-mentioned monthly reports probably omit some standard items considered necessary by your accountant and treasurer. However, the number of so-called necessary reports to be prepared monthly in a foreign office should be held to a minimum. With computer time available, there is a tendency to flood senior management with reams of manifold forms showing infinite detail, which is not very useful and actually a waste of high-cost manhours. One look at a contract status report, a list of accounts receivable, or a graphic showing profit trends should stimulate prompt action from an alert PM.

There is a growing tendency to overanalyze accounting and production reports since the introduction of computer-generated graphics. Engineers sometimes compound this felony (theft of time) by introducing index numbers, such as productivity quotients. These indices vary from firm to firm, and their meaning is usually not well understood in any one organization, so they have no real use in the daily routine of the international PM.

Very often, professionals are lax about collections; they seem inherently to dislike sending invoices to clients. Yet no client is going to pay fees without an invoice. Each contract should contain a payment schedule setting forth percentages of the total fee to be paid upon the delivery of certain documents or after fixed periods of time. Small contracts lasting just a few months might include only an advance payment and a final payment on delivery of the contract documents. Projects of longer duration should provide for either monthly progress payments or substantial payments on delivery of preliminary drawings, on conclusion of reviews by the client's representatives, and on award of individual contracts for construction. International banks and multinationals understand the value of cash and generally are quite amenable to formal payment schedules. It is usually only a matter of proposing one's schedule to the client to get acceptance.

The project manager should supply the accounting department with data to issue invoices and should personally deliver the invoice to the client along with contract documents.

Probably no professional likes to be a bill collector. With international mails noted for being slow and internal distribution in large organizations being worse, there is no substitute for personal delivery of an invoice to a client. Some discretion is advised, but if the invoice is handed to the client in the client's office, there will be no doubt about the fact that the invoice was received. If a foreign language is even remotely involved, the invoice should be in the official language of the client and in the official currency of the contract—no matter what language or currency is used in your accounting system. Don't expect the client to pay a bill in dollars and expressed in English if the contract is in Arabic.

Collections require a carefully planned procedure. It takes some time to learn the processing cycle for invoices in any bureaucracy, and often the help of the local associate is required to learn the approval process. Once this routine is mastered, one of the associate's staff can be assigned to follow the invoice through the trail of "in" baskets. In Latin America, it is worthwhile to have a trusted expediter to "put the invoice back on the top of the pile" if a ministry is having a cash flow problem.

Most clients of architects and engineers intend to pay their bills. Funds for the consultant are normally a line item in international bank financing and in the budget for any large project for a government or an industrial client. If the contract documents have been delivered in good faith, approval and payment may be routine. When feasibility studies or design contracts with individuals are difficult to collect, final resort might be to prepare promissory notes for the balance due, which notes could then be discounted at a bank where the client is known. Presentation of notes to one Middle East client resulted in immediate payment without further discussion. The client was aghast and feigned embarrassment when I presented the notes for signature, but he paid.

Governments are concerned with maintaining their credit rating with international banks. Even when a change of government occurs by coup or revolution, there is great interest in paying outstanding invoices. In Ecuador I once walked into the Ministry of Public Works behind a group of inspectors making a surprise audit of the paymaster. They placed a seal on the safe, so my invoice was "frozen" for a month or so. Yet payment came along in due course—the government had a loan agreement with the World Bank and payment of consultants working on the program was one of the items covered in the agreement.

Along with collection of invoices for services, a consulting firm may occasionally have collection trouble closer to home— for travel funds advanced to staff. International travel is a big item in foreign practice, and employees should not be expected to finance their own business trips. This practice is common domestically, and for short trips where credit cards can be used, there may be no hardship to the employee. A month's trip to Saudi Arabia, however, may cost $5000, and most of that will have to be paid in cash. A system of cash advances for foreign travel should be routine. And it must require employees to make travel expense reports and repay unused cash as soon as they return from their trip. It is slow and difficult sometimes to collect from old and reliable employees after months have elapsed, particularly when outstanding balances grow to more than $1000. So another monthly report essential to good cash management is "Status of Employee Travel Accounts." Horror stories abound—the CEO of one large engineering company was surprised to find several employees who had not completed a travel expense account for over a year which had been full of worldwide travel for these individuals. One way of controlling the expense account problems is to formulate a travel policy and to circulate it to all employees. This policy should be fair and equitable so all employees realize what the travel policy permits. Generally, travel rules will allow some flexibility for long and arduous trips, with senior employees and managers being able to use judgment on choice of accommodations and food costs.

Fixed per diem allowances are often difficult to live with in rapidly developing countries where the only hotels and restaurants acceptable to foreign professionals may be five-star establishments—their rates are higher than those of the best hotels one can find at home. First-class air travel has generally been placed off limits for all but the CEO and the chairperson of the board. Accountants who are watchdogs over these items have little or no foreign travel experience, and so the thought of sitting in an economy-class middle seat on a trip from New York to Dhahran, Saudi Arabia, holds no fears for them.

When there are large numbers of people traveling for extended periods for site surveys, supervision contracts, planning studies, or condition surveys, it may be preferable to establish a flat-rate expense policy. Its purpose is to keep travel expenses from exceeding budgeted amounts while allowing the employee to make his own boarding and lodging arrangements.

Some older companies tend not to publish a travel policy, because certain classes of employees are allowed to treat expense accounts as a perquisite. This practice leads to "dry rot" and is second only to nepotism as a cause for low morale. Publishing travel policy will not only eliminate this practice but also make the matter of travel costs easy to explain to clients.

Travel advances should be examined very carefully. Once in a while an employee may use travel advances as sort of a personal finance plan. This only leads to unpleasantness when time comes to return unused funds. It is usually a trusted and capable employee who gets in this kind of a crisis, which makes the problem more unpleasant for management. Architectural and engineering firms should not be in the personal loan business. One solution might be to help such an employee arrange a bank loan to get through a financial crisis. Such treatment may erase some personal stress and result in a more productive employee.

Wage and salary policy in overseas operations is a definite management problem having no neat or simple solution. Recent years have brought on the scene consulting firms which deal in compensation structures for employees on overseas assignments. Studies are published annually by some on cost-of-living and salary levels in all foreign markets where design firms are active. These consultants and their studies provide guidance, but their real clients are the multinational contractors, manufacturers, and petroleum companies. Such big organizations operate on a much broader profit margin and with less risk than architects, engineers, planners, or construction managers. As a result, the wisest counsel is to be guided by the policy of the competition, which, however, is very difficult to discover. Competing with salary scales of an organization like Aramco would be deadly, so design firms which stay in business abroad treat wage and salary policy decisions very seriously.

Newcomers to the export market frequently adopt a bonus policy, either across the board or by arbitrary selection of recipients. There are stories of cash bonuses being given on the completion of a profitable job, by a partner who handed out packages of cash to the assembled staff at the Christmas party. This must have been a touching scene, but at the end of the fiscal year the senior partner may not have felt so exuberant.

Random bonuses are ill-advised. After the first year, the rank and file will expect bonuses no matter what sort of a financial year the firm experiences. International operations cannot avoid business cycles, which are unpredictable, particularly if there is not a wide client base. So the bonus picture will not always be rosy. A much more satisfying plan for partners, shareholders, and staff is profit sharing—which may take several forms. At the end of each fiscal year a percentage of profit can be set aside for the plan and invested in a separate account. After a few years of participation an employee will have a fully vested interest in a share of the fund, which will be given on resignation or retirement. These funds, when managed by professionals, are very successful and do much for employee morale and stability.

No manager of a large design effort halfway around the world and ten time zones from the office can escape from the concerns of meeting the payroll. One solution might be to have a cash-heavy associate who could bail out the local office on payday until a big invoice is collected. In real life this situation is not very common. A more practical way to have resources in a time of insufficient cash flow is to establish a permanent line of credit at a local bank. This can be done in a number of ways, including a purely local arrangement, using the contract with a client in the country as collateral. This arrangement may be the most economical and efficient method, once a presence has been established and the bank's loan committee does not consider your company a fly-by-night.

An alternative arrangement is for the home office to arrange for a loan to be guaranteed through its own bank, whose correspondent or affiliate bank in the project country will disburse the loan to the local manager. Either of these arrangements provide a security blanket for the PM and work very well.

With proper cash flow forecasting, good invoicing, and solid collection procedures, there should not be a constant need for local credit. Even so, it is good practice to use the credit occasionally after it has been established, to prove that it works and so the deputy manager will know what to do should a crisis arise during the PM's absence. Using your firm's own credit is always preferable to asking the local associate for financial aid, because the odds are that the associate will never understand the reason for not having a few million dollars around somewhere.

Assuming that financial matters are under control and that cash flow predictions show a significant surplus of cash for the next month or so, what should be done with excess funds? Should they be sent to the home office by airmailing a bank draft or by a traveler who happens to be going that way? A cabled bank transfer could be made from the local bank to the home office bank, through banking channels. There are a number of ways to transfer funds, some bad and others worse.

If your bank is one of the large international organizations, like Chase Manhattan, Citibank, Morgan Guaranty, or Barclay's, its telex transfer system could get the funds back to work at home in a day or so. But bankers generally like to use your money as long as they can; for example, when you authorize the transfer on Wednesday or Thursday, the cable does not leave the bank until the next Monday, and the funds may not be in the home office account for ten days. A very reliable way to transfer funds from Europe is by airmail—very often the bank draft will be in your account before a cable transfer would arrive.

If a large sum of money is being transferred, the loss of interest will justify a special messenger's trip. The industry example which will hold the record for years was the trip made to deliver Blount's down payment (over $100 million on its King Faisal University contract) from Riyadh to New York. Chartered plane, Concorde, helicopter, and limousine were all used by a Blount officer racing to get the huge sum back to work and producing interest. Most operations won't be confronted by this horrible problem, but the basic premise is clear. Don't lose the check in the mail!

Financial management of a foreign office is not to be shared by a large group. Engineers and architects have little in their training or practice to equip them for handling the daily details concerning cash management or financial planning. The control should be closely held by two or three officers or partners, each having power of attorney and the trust of the board of directors. They should plan with due regard to company confidentiality, making sure not to bother or panic the staff by open discussion of money problems. Most important, it is very unwise to exhort professionals to redouble efforts to bring a losing project "out of the red" to save the firm from impending bankruptcy. Management usually has to shoulder the blame for such a situation, and passing the blame to the troops will only make matters worse.

In these times of frequently unsettled international relations, currency devaluations, and shaky financial institutions, serious thought should be given to financial security. Besides insurance against risks and losses due to civil wars, riots, and political events, it is prudent management practice to limit cash balances in foreign banks to a modest working level. Cash surpluses should be transferred to the home office account regularly. In addition, if the foreign office is located in an area of unrest, there should be a contingency plan for evacuating staff and dependents by air on short notice. This can be done by giving each head of family the necessary tickets to a safe haven as soon as there are signs of trouble. Cash can be advanced or provided at the destination by a bank or travel agent. Companies like Fluor and Exxon organize these moves with military precision. Plan for security of funds, assets, and staff in any foreign operation.

Although I do not wish to give the impression that the international architectural and engineering business is almost like a wartime operation, I have intended to present a "worst-case scenario" that hammers home the need for careful planning in financial matters. Sound financial leadership and planning is as important as good marketing, a well-developed understanding of other cultures, and high-quality professional work.

A bad financial operation can be identified with a small amount of inspection. Some telltale signs are:

- Financial reports are not current.
- Cost accounting reports lag one or more reporting periods behind the fiscal accounting.

- There is a lack of understanding of the value of work in progress.
- Department heads are not convinced of the importance of meeting budgets.
- There is no clear policy for employee performance ratings and salary reviews.
- Project managers have no concept of profit margins, overhead costs, or manhour requirements for design efforts.
- There is no travel policy or control over the travel budget.
- The top local manager does not accept invoicing and collection as prime responsibilities.

Basic principles that are key to successful financial management of a foreign operation include:

- Send the manager abroad with a good hands-on knowledge of the home office accounting and project reporting system.
- Install a tested contract status reporting system that is understood by senior staff and can be produced on the spot— manually or by microcomputer.
- Define general and office overhead, indoctrinate staff on the items contained in it, and insist on tight overhead control.
- Produce accurate workload estimates.
- Police accounts receivable, and make collection a responsibility of top management.
- Control travel advances and expense accounts carefully.
- Publish travel policy to all members of staff.
- Consider profit sharing plans.
- Establish a line of credit with local banks.
- Develop fast and reliable means of cash transfer.
- Keep foreign cash balances at a modest level.

# CHAPTER 17

# CHANGES, EXTRAS, AND CLAIMS

When a consultant is negotiating the consulting contract, a main objective is that the contract have a well-defined scope of services to be rendered. If the architect-engineer prepares the design contract, control of the amount of detail is retained. Indeed, in domestic practice most contracts with private companies are written by the consultant, unless a standard form prepared by one of the professional societies, such as the American Institute of Architects or the National Society of Professional Engineers, is adapted. In the international field, where many diverse forces are at work, the architect-engineer rarely dictates the contract form.

In general, the contract must be in the language of the client's country and in accordance with the laws and legal practices thereof. If the contract is with a multinational corporation, its bureaucracy, jargon, and legal policy require a special document. Foreign private clients look askance at consultant-prepared drafts of contracts for professional services. So the best one can expect is a chance to assist in defining certain paragraphs by offering the client drafts of schedules, lists of items to be provided (and those not to be provided), a list of specific services to be rendered (as well as those which will not be furnished), and a simple breakdown of the fee by line item or by task. A payment schedule, of course, would be a desirable item to have the client include in your contract, if the client will accept it. Actually, the chances of influencing a foreign government agency to include something of benefit to a consultant in the contract are very slim. But the idea is worth trying.

Once the contract is signed, the PM should isolate the scope of work and continually refer to it until it is known well. When the client requests services not included in the scope, the PM should be able to detect whether this new item is a change or something that the architect-engineer should be doing as a normal part of the design. Often the fee structure of the design contract will govern the decision. If the contract is cost-reimbursable, the client can ask for any changes desired, providing it is realized that the original completion schedule may suffer and that the contract price will increase.

A fixed-price contract usually is structured to have reviews at the concept study stage, at the completion of the preliminary drawings (frequently defined as the final drawings in a 35 percent completion stage), and at the 90 percent completion stage. At each review, certain types of changes can be made without affecting schedule or the consultant's planned level of effort.

Every request of the client should be carefully considered, for the handling of changes in scope will usually set the tone of future relations—if not the success of the contract. But the PM cannot "give away the store." The PM must avoid being "nickled and dimed" into a loss situation by a parsimonious client's representative.

The PM's first reaction on receiving a request for a change should be: Is the item within the scope of work, and if so, is it a change which a professional would expect to make as a routine part of design? If the request is clearly outside the scope of work, the PM should make a detailed fee estimate, including manhours, sheet count, and construction cost estimate, if applicable, as well as an estimate of the effect of this extra work on the design schedule. Armed with this estimate, the PM can determine if the request is one which should be negotiated and made the basis of a claim or accepted as a trading item for past or future reductions in scope.

Often the client will think that the work should be done immediately, before the progress of design or construction makes the change impractical or more costly. The consultant may elect to proceed with the change and to negotiate the change order later. This attitude may make for good client relations, but unless the client has a good record in such affairs, it may not be sound business practice. It would be prudent to get "agreement in principle" in writing as a minimum, before proceeding. Negotiations held after design is complete for changes already accomplished are difficult. The negotiating task might fall to an associate who through lack of background or weakness would be willing to compromise. It is much more satisfactory to complete the necessary amendments to one's contract before proceeding with the design changes.

If the suggested change involves a small amount of design effort yet has real merit and will enhance the project's use or appearance and reduce the cost of construction, the PM may consider accepting the change and using the manhour effort as a swap item in future negotiations. The client is not the only one who dislikes repeated requests for minor items to be added to a contract.

If the scope of work has many "soft" areas (places where the design effort or services to be provided are not definite), the architect-engineer will have considered proposing a feasibility or a concept study earlier on. The client may have insisted on rushing into final design because of time constraints or because it was felt that the architect-engineer should answer all the possible design questions without the client's help or without asking for a fee for the necessary study. Instead of your assuming answers to crucial design criteria and layout matters in such a situation, it is better to force the issue. Design section heads should produce some alternate schemes, with appropriate one-line drawings, and in enough detail to clear the way for preliminary design to proceed without being rejected. A meeting should be arranged with the client's technical representative, preferably in the architect-engineer's design office, to settle the matter and to make decisions on the spot. These drawings should be signed and dated by the PM and the client's authorized representatives. It should be made clear that with this authorization design will proceed to the next milepost and that more changes on the same subject may be cause for a later claim for money or more time.

I suspect that the foregoing procedure may appear to be a bit overbearing—indeed, the PM's patience and sensitivity may be put to a test. But the method works, and when used with good humor and sincerity, it will lead to good client relations.

Such studies can be used at any time during the contract to draw a decision out of an indecisive client. The key is to prepare the case with a minimum of staff effort and to give the client some real options, as well as an idea of the additional cost and time required for design and construction.

Another type of change is worth mentioning—the kind proposed by the architect-engineer, but which the client doesn't appreciate. PMs should investigate those requests that originate from their own staffs with a jaundiced eye. Frequently, a technical supervisor whose section is exceeding the design budget will try to recoup by making such claims. When I took over a design office that had a number of sour contracts, the staff flooded me with such claims. Few of the change orders had any merit, as I discovered when trying to defend the case. It is prudent to examine each claim as objectively as possible before presenting it. Having a reputation as a firm which is continuously making claims against a client is very difficult to overcome.

Proposals for changes in scope of work should be presented promptly and completely. The alert PM will put the case together and advise the client that a claim is being considered. No client likes a bombshell to be dropped without warning, and good relations can be protected by using a diplomatic approach. There are often compelling reasons why a client cannot amend a contract, and consideration should be given to the client's position. It may be that another ministry is involved or that it is not politically expedient to ask for an increase in a project's cost at the time. The matter might be settled by a trade-off—reducing the scope of work in some other area.

If the client wants a very costly and extensive change in design, the contract should provide a course for remedy, such as arbitration or use of the local courts. This is where competent local and international legal assistance could be required. Fortunately, these cases do not occur often on design contracts in the export market. In my experience, settlements have always been negotiated for design squabbles, except in cases where one side furnished false or erroneous information or a stubborn individual wanted to go to court to prove a point.

Negotiations for change orders should follow the pattern established by the proposals and negotiations for the main contract. Unless wages and salaries have increased drastically, the basic contract rates will govern. Many contracts require the maintenance of prices for all changes resulting in increases of less than 20 percent (for example) of the original contract price.

The big question concerns what is extra to the effort originally intended. Careful documentation and care are required. No architect-engineer ever got rich or famous on change orders, so the negotiations should be settled promptly.

Claiming compensation for extra work during planning, design, and construction supervision is vastly different from seeking compensation for a change in the scope of design. For example, extra work might be described as an extension or an addition to the contract. In a contract for highway design, the client may extend the length of the project by 50 percent. An urbanization project might be increased to add another subdivision or neighborhood. Transmission line design could be added to a contract for design of a hydroelectric project. These are examples of extra work which a client may want to award to an architectural and engineering firm because it is already on the site, has a good understanding of the environment, and is qualified to provide the service. The owner is likely to get a good contract price because of these circumstances. The consultant will benefit from the understanding of the client and familiarity with the contract documents already prepared. A proposal will be simple to prepare as an extension to the present contract. Negotiation will probably be simplified if there is no large increase in salaries or overheads. In addition, this new extra work contract is just as good as one from a new client, and has been sold without any real marketing effort, which can make it more profitable. A large extra work contract is a long stride toward winning repeat business, which for obvious reasons is very attractive in the international market.

The scope of services to be provided for extra work should be described in just as specific a manner as in the original contract. If design drawings used on the basic contract are to be used as typical designs for the extra work, extreme care should be taken.

Site-adapting an existing design to a new location, for example, must be studied in detail because of foundation conditions, orientation, location of utilities, and access roads. The client will not be overjoyed with a charge for using standard details and specifications again, because of feeling that this has already been paid for on the basic contract. At home, we thought the drawings belonged to the architect-engineer, but now we learn that in the export business, the client owns the designs. (The client is probably already planning to use the designs for another project after we leave!) So the proposal for extra work should be well thought out and must be negotiated carefully.

Just the fact of being on the site and having an ongoing design contract will expose the architect-engineer to requests for "free" consulting of all descriptions. These requests should be referred to the PM, because only the latter should be in control. Requests for personal service are not easy to handle. Designing a country home for the client's chief engineer, for example, could be discussed and probably turned down without dire consequences. A tennis court for the minister or the interior design of the director's office might be another matter.

Even the most organized of clients, with the strictest rules of conduct, are not shy about proposing "extra work" on their contracts. Usually the leak starts at the bottom of the staff and is the result of friendly environment, not any real sense of wrongdoing. For example, a resident electrical engineer was frequently talked into providing free design for various items which should have been contract change orders. Being a "good fellow" and absolutely without malice, he would do this engineering on his own time, at no cost to the owner. By his own way of rationalizing, the free work would make for better client relations. But the ramifications were too numerous to mention.

If the architect-engineer gives something to a client, it should be included in the contract and subject to all the guarantees and remedies provided.

The PM's task will be to interpret requests and decide whether or not to claim an extra if the work is not clearly included in the scope. The decision making is very difficult to define. A fairly good rule might be, in the absence of all other guidance, "Lose the little ones and win the big ones!" If the request is related to the project and is for a task, such as additional surveying or design of more facilities similar to those included in the scope of services, the proposal should be made and payment sought. The extent of the fight expended in negotiations for the proposed fee may become a matter of an administrative or business decision.

In a European setting—with an engineer or contractor from the continent—one may expect low original bids with extravagant claims for extras beginning the first day of work or shortly after the contract is signed. The practice not only extends to contractors but engineers as well. European professionals usually delay their invoicing until the job has been finished and then include the extras in the "annual" bill. By that time the details are blurred, and the urgency has gone. This approach has been perfected by centuries of tradition. Companies with cash flow predictions to be met and balance sheets to prepare cannot operate successfully for long by depending on change orders and extravagant claims. One should be aware and continue to be amused but be guided by more pragmatic policies.

The Arab culture, which may vary somewhat between regions, requires another approach to claims and extra work. In my experience, there is a general feeling that "a deal is a deal," and after the contract price is fixed, it should not be changed. The amount of services to be provided by the architect-engineer is assumed to be unlimited—everything it takes to design the project described in the contract. To be fair about it, there are many contributing factors which make this position understandable, if not wholly acceptable. American ways of designing, contracting, construction, and business systems were thrust on the Middle East in the 1960s, resulting in a culture shock unparalleled in history. Many business deals in that area have been less than scrupulous. Arab clients are very cautious, and their new professionals have inherited this wary attitude in dealing with outsiders. So a fixed-price contract with a Middle East government will be very difficult, if not impossible, to change. Additions and deletions to the scope of work are negotiated by trading rather than price changes. Their system works both ways, because if the work effort is lessened, one will rarely be asked to lower the fee. In several cases, I have seen examples of the Arab's kind of compensation—new contracts awarded or changes made to involve extra work at very favorable prices—to cover increase of effort or obvious losses suffered on previous contracts. The first time this happened I could not believe my interpretation of the facts. It is true that with trust and confidence established, the Arab position will be very fair. This fairness will not be expressed in our way but in accordance with their tradition and culture. The test of time is in play here, and overnight action is not to be expected.

Dealing with change orders and extra work revisions for architectural and engineering contracts in the international market is thus considerably different from domestic practice. The design professional's world abroad is much less litigious and more flexible than in the construction contractor's arena either at home or abroad. Legal advice is most important during any proposal preparation and contract negotiation, but help must be selected with care. The lawyer chosen must be aware of language, cultural, and traditional differences, as well as the legal system of the client's country. A lawyer in your locality who traveled once or twice to the project area or whose ancestors came from abroad does not thereby necessarily qualify as a good source of legal assistance. A number of international law offices specialize in geographical areas of the world—there are even a few who know the needs of the design professions. Well-qualified legal help is the only kind to summon to the international scene.

Good communications between the PM and the client and the involvement of the local associate as a party to the contract are essential to the efficient handling of change orders and extra work and to minimizing problems of interpretation of the contract. As soon as a scope change is suspected, the PM should get on record with the client. Agreement in principle on the changes and the effect on the architect-engineer fee should be obtained before any effort is expended on the change. Extra work contract revisions should be handled as new contracts and should be treated with great discretion. One should *not* begin extra work without a negotiated and signed agreement, with all the guarantees that were required for the basic contract. Due regard to these principles will contribute to a PM's longevity.

There comes a time in international planning, architectural, and engineering practice when the only solution to a dispute seems to be a claim against a client for some injury—real or imagined. In fact, there may appear to be no other way to get the client's attention than to make a claim and demand the remedies provided by the contract. Such cases are few and far between because making or threatening to make such a claim damages the client-professional relationship. Before such a claim is presented, one must anticipate the probable loss of the client and must evaluate this loss. If the claim results from some default by the client—where information necessary to the design process was not furnished or was not complete—the consequence might have been to require the consultant to expend two or three times the number of manhours that had been proposed to finish the contract.

A planning contract with the U.S. Air Force offers a classic example of nonexistence of essential information. A number of firms were short-listed for updating the master plans of foreign American air bases. The existing plans and photographs were gathered together in one room—tons of material—and the short-listed firms were invited to send representatives to inspect the information. The request for proposal (RFP) made reference to the material, but the mountain of paper could not be evaluated in the time allotted. A proposal was submitted on assumptions made after talking with the client's representative, reading the RFP, and a day's visit to the assembled references. As soon as the contract got underway, it became obvious that the material supplied had not been properly understood or evaluated by the client and that the scope of work was in error. The contract was completed under protest, but the architect-engineer had to expend about double the effort in manhours and travel expense that had been proposed. Happily, in this case the client recognized the problem, and the claim received fair treatment.

Other cases of claims by architectural and engineering firms against clients in developing countries, in my experience, are often rooted in similar causes. Information promised in contracts either was nonexistent or incomplete. In particular, the survey fieldwork done by the client's forces or contract surveyors may not meet the standards of accuracy claimed in the contract. Plan and profile sheets of ongoing projects may exist but not in any usable form. In one case a 2-meter-long sheet was presented as a final drawing for about 200 kilometers of mountain highway. The client had said that plans for the project were ready to go to contractors for bidding purposes!

Claims against governments in rapidly developing countries are usually self-defeating. In one country, when the president was told that a major contractor for a hydroelectric project was planning to make a claim, he allegedly said, "Tell him to go ahead. The contract says he must make the claim in our courts, and I appoint the judges!"

A better way of preserving your sanity and the financial health of your company is to make a thorough investigation before committing the proposal effort.

On the subject of claims, the contracting procedure should involve international arbitration. In countries where laws require use of local courts, one should determine whether an unusual risk is being taken by pursuing a claim through litigation. Saudi Arabia, for example, has such a law, but the courts are regarded as very fair to foreign contractors. Arbitration is an alternative to litigation that may reduce the cost in terms of money, time, and public embarrassment.

The problem is to assemble an international staff which can

investigate projects and appraise its organization's ability to complete the design profitably. One firm's reaction to the RFP, even after a site visit, may be wholly negative, while an experienced team from another firm may return from the project country enthusiastic about the opportunity and the prospect of working with the client's staff. This difference of opinion often relates to international experience, good project management, and committed management. Some firms adapt to the international market; others never solve its riddles.

When performing construction management and supervision, the international architectural and engineering firm may become exposed to contractors' claims. The words "may become" are used because during my long career in international engineering and construction, none of my experience with claims reached the point where a lawsuit was initiated. All claims were settled by negotiation, and only a handful reached that stage.

But it is a fact that the engineering-construction business is becoming more litigious, and this practice may spread into the international field. Arbitration can be a much more practical route for settlement of international claims for reasons of time, expense, the possibility of a fair settlement, and privacy.

The subject of construction claims, lawsuits, and arbitration has been covered comprehensively in recent engineering literature. The second edition of *International Construction Contracts,* by McNeill Stokes, is an excellent source of guidance for entrants to the export market.

The scarcity of lawsuits in the international architect-engineer's daily routine does not indicate that there are never any disputes or arguments. The nature of overseas contracts tends to produce areas of misunderstanding for clients and consultants alike. Communications breakdowns, or the lack of understanding of the other person's language and culture, are the main underlying causes of disputes, but there are many other potential causes. The most effective preventative of disputes in professional service contracts is an open two-way line from consultant to client. Of all the duties and responsibilities assigned to the PM, this is the most important. There is no trade-off for the ability to communicate. A PM who cannot arrange a way to communicate with a foreign client is a liability who will lead to disaster.

The alert PM will organize a simple system to keep track of daily happenings of significance to the design contract. Logs, diaries, reports of telephone conversations, tickler files, photos, coordination meetings, and status reports will all play a role. The PM will be guided by the inverse to the saying "No news is good news." In the international consulting business no news is bad news. Regular contact with the client, whether or not there is any big problem to discuss, is the key to avoidance of trouble. The client expects to have an opportunity to hear about progress on the project and a chance to be recognized. The PM will provide this contact by telex, telephone, and, above all, by periodic visits.

In addition to routine visiting, the PM should be the person who talks to the client about potential problems and disputes—maybe even claims, as soon as they surface. Of course, the good news is always easy to deliver. The "bad news" messenger role is more difficult, and may cause client displeasure and even worse. The PM must learn the art of presenting solutions to bad problems and that requests for more time and more fees are not the only viable options.

Potential claims, arbitration, and lawsuits will bring the peerless PM to understand what mental stress is all about. For example, many design organizations have developed a philosophy for conduct in claims involving professional liability which counsels project managers not to talk to the client. One can imagine the reactions of an international client who has developed a working relationship with an international vice president or PM of the consultant over several years when that person says, "Our legal adviser tells me not to discuss the roof leaks with you." This attitude will do little to promote repeat business. Keep the lines of communication, which were so carefully planned and built, in an open state.

Some principles for dealing with changes, extra work, and claims follow.

- Study the scope of work—commit it to memory.
- Consider the client's requests for changes in scope very carefully and make a detailed estimate of their cost and time effect.
- Use concept studies to refine the scope of work and to "freeze" the design criteria.
- Examine objectively staff-originated change orders.
- Regard change orders as an opportunity to add to workload without any marketing effort.

- Beware requests for "free" work.
- Lose the little ones and win the big ones.
- Don't expect extra work claims for design changes to impress Middle East clients.
- International consulting operates in a less litigious and more flexible climate than domestic practice.
- Choose an international lawyer who knows your client's country, language, and culture well.
- Construction claims usually have little in common with claims relating to design contracts.
- Communication between client and consultant is paramount. Select, appoint, and train PMs who have the stuff to maintain client communications.
- No news is bad news.

## CHAPTER 18

# POLITICS, BRIBERY, ET CETERA

The first mention of foreign projects to a domestically oriented audience probably will elicit remarks about bribery and corruption. It is a widespread belief that international consulting is different from domestic practice because of large doses of politics, which inevitably lead to bribery and corruption. So it comes as a shock to many to learn the truth—that these ingredients do not permeate foreign consulting and construction contracts any more than might be the case at home.

I recall being introduced to an audience at the University of Wisconsin, in Milwaukee, by a speaker who said, "He has had long experience in international projects and knows all about bribery and corruption." His remark took me by surprise. The subject is difficult to discuss, but I believe one must address corruption when discussing international practice if only to dispel wrong impressions.

Politics is another matter. All government-sponsored programs have considerable political content. Infrastructure projects in developing countries, such as ports, highways, airports, and water and sewer systems, are political by nature, and their proponents have generally tried for years to attract foreign aid in terms of grants and loans. Foreign aid in itself is a political weapon and, therefore, often involves the consultant—unwittingly—in local politics. When signing a contract to design a road system or a hydroelectric project for a foreign government, the consultant tacitly accepts a role in helping his client defend the program from political attack. If the program runs over budget, is delayed during construction, or runs into legal problems of expropriation of private property, the consultant can expect to become involved in support of the client. As long as one can maintain professional independence and serve the client in a staff position, this activity is regarded as a typical requirement of professional practice.

It is discreet to stay aloof from partisan politics in another culture. No foreigner should allow himself to be placed in a Machiavellian role by the client, even when the security blanket of an international lending agency seems very protective. If politics at home in a democracy seem complicated, imagine the challenges offered by the situation a consultant meets in a developing country. And yet the client will often need engineering support to defend decisions taken on infrastructure programs. Questions will arise concerning route location, equipment purchasing, personnel selection, and budgets. The consultant's PM will be the obvious choice to play the part of buffer against public criticism. The following examples illustrate ways the client may call on the PM for political support.

- The route of a major federal highway relocation required the removal of dozens of ancient royal poinciana trees in the median of a boulevard which was being widened. The PM was selected by the client to address irate garden club members and other groups to explain the reasons for removing these grand old trees. (The project site was in the United States.) The right-of-way of this project passed through a long row of one-story frame houses rented on a weekly basis to low-income families. The owner of these miserable buildings was a friend of the consulting firm's senior partner. Both being fellow members of the symphony orchestra board, the real estate tycoon tried to influence the engineering firm to move the project center line so his buildings would be spared. The PM was again the logical person to explain the facts of life about highway location to the influential landlord.

- A World Bank highway program in Ecuador involved projects of much greater size and difficulty than ever attempted in that country. Kilometers of deep rock excavation in the Andes mountain system required machinery and methods not known to local contractors. The consultant was given the task of pre-qualifying local firms who would then be able to work with the successful international bidders as subcontractors. Generally, these local contractors were accustomed to using hand labor. Their equipment lists included thousands of picks and shovels, a few tents, pickup trucks, and lots of wheelbarrows (not the self-propelled type). The PM eventually devised some questions and tests to assist in identifying qualified companies, whose owners were all political supporters of the president of the republic. One of the questions which helped eliminate the unfit involved asking a candidate to study a picture of a gigantic land-slide on the Pan American Highway in Guatemala and to outline a plan for removal of the slide.

■ The government agency in charge of a hydroelectric project being built with a World Bank loan had a large engineering staff—sort of a mini-TVA. The first qualification for employ-ment as an engineer was apparently membership in the ruling party. One of the World Bank's requirements before approving the loan was for the agency to employ a construction manage-ment adviser to bolster the inexperienced staff. The president of the republic periodically called on the adviser for confidential performance ratings for his national engineers—another unex-pected role for a consultant.

The PM frequently gets placed in a position of being pres-sured into making judgments and of having to give support not included in the job description and probably totally outside of any previous experience. The problem often arises unexpect-edly and in an innocent way.

I was having dinner with some friends in a Quito restaurant late one stormy evening when I was interrupted by a driver from the Ministry of Public Works bearing a very official-looking doc-ument. There was a statement for my signature, as PM, that the ministry's highway department had studied a large number of alternate routes through the mountains for a certain project and that the route chosen by the consultant and the World Bank was the same route recommended originally by the min-istry. Suspecting some larger controversy, probably in the press, I sent the minister a message saying I had no knowledge of the problem but would be happy to help him with a report when our team had looked at the facts. The next day the minister thanked me but apparently the crisis went away because he did not pursue the matter.

The consulting engineer gets placed on the griddle by a variety of people seeking information about the project. Loan agencies and international banks frequently ask for details about the project, data they have been unable to obtain from the borrower through normal channels. This action again will place the PM in an uneasy position, because very often his reputation as a competent professional may be at stake. Acting as an undercover agent for a lending agency or for one's own government is an unrewarding task and could result in antagonizing everyone concerned. An alert PM will entertain requests from third parties with extreme caution to protect his professional reputation.

Consulting firms involved in foreign work seem to attract "agents," confidence men, information brokers, and gratuitous help more than any other organization in the design field. It is difficult to remember that the export market is not the only place where the "victors get the spoils." Perhaps because other languages and customs are involved, and grade B spy thrillers have their settings in romantic places like Paris, Rome, Istanbul, and Hong Kong, the public seems to expect international projects to have a bribery and corruption content. The attitude is nourished by basic differences in culture, economic conditions, and perceptions of other societies.

For example, a person who automatically adds 15 percent to a restaurant bill as a tip at home will frequently refuse to understand that service charges in foreign restaurants do not always go to the waiters. In some countries, one must tip for personal services at every turn. The local people understand and accept this system, while a tourist may never understand the customs—or will respond lavishly and carelessly, becoming an object of ridicule. The custom of *baksheesh* in the Middle East and *dash* in Nigeria frequently impresses the foreigner as just another attack on his dignity when, in fact, the custom probably stems from another concept of charity. For one to get baggage from behind the counter in many international airports or to get suitcases from one's room to the hotel lobby, small sums have to change hands. Otherwise, there will be embarrassing moments, no movement, and lots of temper displayed.

The next step in this culture gap may be something called "grease"—by our own peculiar western standards, something between a tip and a bribe. These are the favors which seem to fuel good service—more attention than given to those who ignore local customs. The telex operator in a Middle East hotel will react to kind words, patience, and block printing of long messages. If one adds to this, on the first use of the telex in a new hotel, a sizable tip (grease) along with the kind words, the system seems to work fine. A small present brought from home will be very well received in places where gifts are customary. South African and Iranian friends, for example, always seemed to have some thoughtful personal gift for departure time, a custom of the culture. Italian and German business acquaintances invariably come to dinner with flowers for the hostess. A modest amount of attention, discussion, and study of other customs will help understanding of tipping, presents, *baksheesh, dash,* and the cultural importance of each.

In the international business world, there may be a culture whose practices will be offensive. For example, in a bankrupt country where poverty, starvation, and theft are rampant, an affluent foreigner is fair game. One's first reaction is to take on all the charity cases of the world and to try to help everyone. After some bitter experiences, like discovering panhandlers and petty criminals, one will adopt a cynical approach and restrict charity to proven cases. In such a climate, public servants will be very poorly paid, often very proud, and sometimes corrupt. Expediting paperwork through bureaucratic agencies, paying taxes, and getting customs clearances may be a major obstacle race. Very often, the only way to get an invoice to the top of the pile or a decision on the amount of customs fees due on a shipment will involve a discreet tip, that is, *dash* or grease. This is no place for a PM to be establishing new standards and customs. A trusted local employee, preferably one of the office administrators who understands local customs and kind words, should be relied upon to preserve the company image and reputation.

Bribery, in spite of all the dire warnings of your friends at home, if encountered abroad, will come as a big surprise. But anyone who reads the newspapers and watches TV at home will know that no country has a monopoly on bribery. Giving something of value to an appointed or elected official to make a decision in one's favor is a crime in any culture and has no place in our discussions. Travelers are prone to interpret their own actions more leniently as they get further from home base, but the rules on bribery don't change very much. What was wrong at home is just as wrong in Africa.

As mentioned earlier, consulting firms seem to have a great attraction for sellers of uranium mines, introductions to the brother of the prime minister, and the head of the secret police. The best protection from these parasites is a smile, a wave, and a hasty exit. Many times what these "fixers" offer to do can be best done by oneself and with little or no effort, as the following examples illustrate:

■ In Libya, an American lawyer offered to represent a firm for a modest retainer. After agreement, the lawyer introduced a person who later became the firm's local associate. When asked to perform some simple legal services, the lawyer demurred, saying that his retainer was for making the one introduction. Such help is not needed—engage lawyers as legal advisers.

■ A Miami contractor met an American from Guatemala who offered to find a local associate with the proper connections to land a large Guatemalan highway construction contract. Two weeks and several thousand dollars later, the contractor discovered that his trip to Guatemala had been in vain, that there were no local associates with anything to offer, and no highway program contemplated. That learning experience had a high tuition.

■ A senior partner in a design firm met a fellow tourist who introduced himself as an associate of an ex-CIA officer with "connections" in several Middle East countries. After much wasted discussion, the PM found out that his own firm's track record in the Middle East was better than that of the retired agent, whose use in marketing professional services was not only very questionable but worthless.

In short, in the international market, a newcomer wanting to associate with questionable characters will find the "opportunities" abroad no less numerous than at home. There are sound methods of selecting an associate in Chapter 5, and one should not be enticed away from this rational approach by visions of romance, dark alley encounters, and sudden riches. Standards which served well in developing a professional reputation at home should not be abandoned in foreign operations.

In spite of stories of intrigue and corruption encountered by others in negotiating or administering foreign contracts, there are surprises that give the lie to the cynics. In Libya, our client, executive director of a government agency, was a design professional educated at a conservative eastern U.S. university. Excellent relations existed between us and this client. Our contract was proceeding nicely. One day, in a relaxed conversation on the job site, the director told me how pleased he was with our contractual relations. Most of all, he said, the fact that our firm had exhibited good business ethics pleased him greatly. He went on to relate that many international firms seemed to abandon their values when they left their home base and that as far as he personally was concerned he would not approve of a contract with any such firm.

Experiences on international construction contracts, particularly in a new culture, are not all without amusement. Our highway project in Ecuador went through a rich coffee-producing region. The final alignment had not been chosen and considerable pressure was being exerted by the big landowners, who wanted the highway near their property so their produce could be hauled to market on large trucks, rather than by mule train. One day a very elegant female landowner was ushered into my office to plead her case for moving the highway alignment closer to her plantation. Making her last desperate pitch, she asked, "Do you like coffee, Señor Ingeniero?" "Yes," I replied, "I often drink three or four cups a day." "No, no, no," she exclaimed, "I am not talking about cups—I'm talking about trees. If the road comes to our farm, we will give you a grove of trees that will produce an income for a long time!" Alas, no farm for me in the Andes—but an intriguing idea!

On the subjects of tax assessment and collection, stories used to abound about fixers and negotiators. But tax reform has taken place over the years in many areas. There are now international accountants and tax lawyers in the capital of a developing country. A design firm with contracts in a new market should take advantage of these able advisers to clarify its tax obligations. In fact, using the same careful approach as one might employ at home will serve as well in the developing countries and thus help avoid the less-than-scrupulous opportunists who might try to take advantage of foreign firms. In questions of local taxes, there is no substitute for the best available counsel. The foreign firm should be forewarned that it is a prime target for so-called tax consultants, the local government's tax advisers, and just plain scoundrels.

It is one matter to protect the integrity of personal reputation and quite another to take on the policing of public morality. A consultant supervising a contract financed by the World

Bank, for example, has not only a contractual obligation to the client, the borrower, but a professional obligation to the client, the bank, and to himself.

The goal is to see that a high-quality project is delivered on schedule and within budget. In the process, the consulting engineer will be taxed to understand everything that is going and to resolve constant questions of ethics, cultural differences, and morality.

It is easy to revert to judging local people by one's own standards. In the course of these experiences, many Americans forget "Watergate," construction and engineering scandals, and the existence of shoddy business practices at home. A friend in Ecuador once said, only half jokingly, "It may take you some time to change the contractors in this area. The conquistadores poured molten gold down their victim's throats and even that didn't work." Each PM will have to develop a personal code of ethics and regulate his conduct accordingly. If the hiring practices of the local government sometimes seem too pragmatic, try to remember how the U.S. secretary of transportation gets selected. Stick with your own code of conduct. Imposing it on other cultures may produce ulcers for you.

In most of the world, business is done with friends. Just as we trade favors with friends in our society, the practice exists in the international construction market. And unhampered by the IRS, the General Accounting Office, or antitrust laws, these favors sometimes affect the award of huge contracts. An outsider may look on such favoritism as unacceptable business conduct. Yet how, for example, does one get to be appointed U.S. ambassador to England?

The PM will be charged with making decisions about favors, tips, and grease as a daily routine. Occasionally, until the word gets around about the PM's principles, there will be confrontation with someone who offers or demands a bribe. Once these issues have been carefully weighed and a policy established, the staff, the business community, and the client will begin to understand the PM's (and the consulting firm's) standards. When this happens, life will become more predictable and the job at hand will be less subject to interruption by unacceptable proposals. The alternative to not taking a clear stand on bribery and other issues of morality in business is that one's office will be a target for all the confidence games in the area.

Although local politics may seem romantic and intriguing, the international consultant should keep clear. Acting as an engineering adviser to the client, who may be a high government official and thus an active politician, will be politics enough. This staff function must be carried out professionally, not covertly, and without participation in local political activity.

The international consultant must establish personal rules of conduct, keep out of local politics, and furnish the very best professional effort that his organization can provide for the client. Maintenance of personal and corporate reputation should be the number one priority.

## CHAPTER 19

# WARS, MILITARY COUPS, AND TERRORISM

Developing countries provide foreign consultants with a great variety of challenges, experience, and special risks. Few developing countries with great infrastructural needs or new wealth from natural resources have stable governments that are established by free elections. They can expose the consultant to unmeasurable risks of unstable government and military rule. When one comes from a stable democracy, the prospect of working under the jurisdiction of a military dictatorship is abhorrent.

Design consultants nevertheless do operate in places such as Greece, Cyprus, Lebanon, Libya, El Salvador, and Nigeria, where daily life may become war-torn or at least dangerously unsettled. Usually, the lure of foreign travel and overseas bonuses overcomes minor inconveniences suffered by expatriate staff due to cultural and environmental climates. As long as the job remains profitable and employee morale good, the home office management has no qualms about the contract.

But when payments lag or families have to be evacuated because of civil strife ("Yankee go home"), concern begins to grow. Board members will then ask, "Why are we working in Bangladesh, anyway?"

Usually, however, management will be content to hang on or ignore the situation until the PM's patience is exhausted. In practice, this rarely happens, so the project goes on in spite of local events and escalating risks. For even in unsettled times, the client will make a good-faith effort to pay the consultant's fees, because the debt is a foreign account and foreign credit is important to developing countries. If payments to foreign contractors and consultants are stopped, the world's bankers immediately become alarmed. In addition, design and construction will grind to a halt and expatriate staff will leave. The complete stoppage of projects has not happened very often, except in situations such as occurred in Iran in 1975 and 1976 and, more recently, in Argentina when overspending and inflation brought projects to a standstill. Under these conditions, marketing for new contracts is useless, and the consultant is intent on completing, collecting, and getting out.

Changes in government are a common event in the international consultant's life. When one signs a contract in a country where political risk is a factor, military coups should come as no surprise. Insurance for political and economic risk can be obtained from the Overseas Private Investment Corporation (OPIC) for certain countries and from private insurers, like Lloyd's of London, for those not covered by OPIC. Because the insurance usually covers each separate invoice, it can be dropped when considered unnecessary.

The consultant should select staff with extreme care for a contract with a high risk factor. The PM must be a known quantity, a person who will keep the staff from panic when the rumors start. In Latin America, for example, changes of government by military coup have averaged one per year in several countries. So a change may cause inconvenience and wasted effort but not much personal stress. We were visiting Quito, Ecuador, when friends advised us to leave on a certain Friday. When questioned, they said, "The opposition will take over the government on Saturday afternoon. It has been agreed with the archbishop that the wedding of the president's daughter at noon on Saturday will not be disturbed, but there will be a change of government after the ceremony." We left on Friday.

Not all changes are as well coordinated as the above Ecuadorian caper, but the consultant's work usually goes on— with perhaps a change in the minister having authority over the project. If the project is financed by an international lending agency, there may be hardly a ripple. Even in Libya, consulting contracts were continued during the Arab-Israeli war of 1967. Some consultants evacuated families, but the government refused to admit that anything unusual had happened. No claims were allowed for the extra cost of evacuation because the client said there was no reason for moving dependents. In Greece there were several periods under the Papadopolous regime ("The Colonels' Government," 1970 to 1975) when martial law including curfews was imposed. But business proceeded as usual. Beirut, Lebanon, in a continuous state of unrest since 1967, has, however, been a sad experience for many foreign consultants.

Experience in Lebanon, Iran, Nigeria, Iraq, and Libya has taken a big toll on the interest of U.S. engineers, architects, and planners in international practice and has sent many experienced internationalists to seek quieter markets. Professionals of other exporting nations—particularly British, French, and Italians—take a less alarmed view toward wars and civil strife. Probably their European heritage has prepared them to accept violent change better than Americans, and they are more inclined to wait patiently for calmer times. Frequently, British staff, for example, have manned contracts for U.S. design firms after the U.S. nationals have been evacuated.

Consulting contracts have been carried to completion in spite of unsettled conditions with notable exceptions. When unrest has led to a shooting war, terrorism, inflation, and disruption of normal life, the market has of course disappeared. A prudent consultant will evaluate these changing conditions carefully, aided by input from foreign associates and their own managers on the scene. The key is to pull out of the market without financial loss or, at least, to cut losses as soon as they appear inevitable. This philosophy will be discussed at greater length in the final chapter. The purpose of this discussion is not to propose a Pollyannish view of the effects of unstable governments and dictatorships on choice of clients. Rather, the consultant considering an international market must develop a system of thorough evaluation so that all risks can be estimated properly. If staff work is incomplete or poorly presented, any given foreign venture in an unstable country will have little chance of success. Foreign affairs are rarely understood by the general public, and design professionals are no exception.

A board of directors uncommitted to export will squelch new ventures without being fully informed. If a firm operates on the basic principle that "if you don't go near the water, you will never get wet,'' it cannot possibly maintain a commitment to foreign operations.

Unless one is a defense contractor and working for his own government, the person would be foolhardy to attempt to operate a foreign design office in a war zone. I was involved in establishing and staffing a large design office in Beirut in 1975. Caught in the crossfire before opening day, the building was a total loss and the office was never occupied. Despite a great amount of study and planning, many foreign firms including oil companies and design-constructors were caught in the war and forced to move their headquarters out of the country.

Granted that attractive opportunities are often found in unstable surroundings, the prudent consultant can take advantage of the steps outlined in Chapter 2 for evaluating political and security risks. Advisers should be chosen with great care, because some of them have no experience with the design or construction world. The rationale for keeping a Beirut embassy open has nothing to do with the conduct of a design operation.

A consultant qualified to evaluate political risks should have a good understanding of the contract scope. Choose wisely, however, because few former diplomats or intelligence officers have this background.

The prospect of financial and professional reward, as well as the outlook for a continuing workload, should be markedly greater as risks increase. Otherwise the problem is reduced to absurdity—would the investment be more profitable if the money were placed in certificates of deposit?

In addition to increased profit margins, the staff should be handpicked from proven professionals who have satisfactory records in hardship posts. The PM should be an ''unflappable'' type who can live without dependents and through long periods of silence from the home office.

Evaluation of consultant's operations in Saigon, Vietnam, and in Lagos, Nigeria, provide a sharp contrast in PMs. The Saigon office, which served the Department of Defense, operated under wartime conditions with a minimum of problems. Good professional services were provided and the client was content. Even a rocket attack which destroyed the unoccupied office was survived without difficulty. The PM, after a shakedown period, organized a staff of veterans who knew how to protect themselves and to survive.

At the other extreme, the Lagos operation was a complete disaster. The representative stationed there devoted most of his time to personal survival with little attention to professional problems. Home office support was lacking, and the budget was insufficient to provide either a decent company image or an adequate protection of personnel. The company representative lived in constant fear of robbery and violence in an unprotected apartment and became ineffective professionally. Recommendations were made to close the operation and to abandon the market.

In Panama, a farm-to-market planning, design, and supervision contract was carried out over a four-year period marked by political unrest. The contract with the Ministry of Public Works was financed by a World Bank loan, and work went along with no unusual problems that could be attributed to the demonstrations, student marches, and frequent stone-throwing incidents at the American Embassy. The work force, predominantly Panamanian, maintained high morale and excellent production. Occasionally there were messages left on our doors saying "Yankee go home" in several graphic ways, and the newspapers and TV carried much anti-American propaganda. But, as usual, there was a hostile political party line and a very friendly private personal relationship with our Panamanian friends. On rare occasions, when a student demonstration was planned, we closed the design office for a half-day and sent everyone home. Work in the interior on project sites was never affected by those events. Moreover, the Panama experience was in keeping with that in other unsettled countries, such as Nigeria and Greece. Press reports to the outside world, in most cases, overemphasized turmoil and inconvenience. Efforts by local governments to contain the unrest and to protect the lives and property of the public received no mention.

There are times when foreign governments are confronted by the outrage and grief of their citizens, and must allow some public expression to surface. In Lagos, Nigeria, in 1975, after President Murtallah Mohammed was assassinated, mobs took to the streets and marched on the U.S. and British embassies. The police were everywhere, mixing with the crowds, attempting to prevent rioting and bodily harm. In one case, the mob surrounded a visitor's taxi and was about to remove him from the vehicle, when a young unarmed policeman prevailed on the students to calm down. Later discussions with Nigerian friends disclosed that the police often used the tactic of allowing the public to "blow off steam," to reach calm in this overcrowded, hot, and squalid city, where tensions seem to run high even under good conditions. To an outsider, the mob scene was menacing, and it is certain that the media's embroidery aggravated the situation.

Life under a dictator who maintains relations with foreign powers can be a disquieting experience. But such governments need to borrow money from international lending agencies and also to get loans and grants from friendly countries. This financial activity generates work for consultants, and the projects have to be staffed with some foreign professionals. A contract in one of these countries can be rewarding to an organization but may apply heavy stress to the principles of the PM and staff. In general terms, if the project is funded by the World Bank, the borrower has mortgaged its country (or part of it) to the Bank in exchange for a loan to build highways, ports, or hydroelectric plants. The Bank usually has made an in-depth investigation of business practices, engineering capability, and income available to service the loan. Severe restrictions will have been placed on the borrower, in the form of requiring auditors, engineering consultants, and construction managers. These advisers are placed on the borrower's payroll and paid out of the loan proceeds. The arrangement helps make the experts almost untouchable, and they are considered to be unofficial employees of the lending agency.

In such a role, one leads an almost charmed life in an otherwise repressive country. The existence of house arrests, interrogations, police brutality, and surveillance are things that one hears rumors about but may not see unless there is an inadvertent meeting with some of the opposition party. Countries in this condition have martial law, curfews, and checkpoints manned by armed soldiers.

Any staff provided by the government is made up of loyal party members. These types have been known to report all actions of foreigners. In these circumstances, telephones are tapped and privacy invaded in numerous ways. Yet some expatriates can exist seemingly unperturbed in this atmosphere. Generally, foreign professionals are not affected and the umbrella of the lending agency provides fine protection. In my experience, most troubles in this kind of setting come from incompetent and overbearing officials who are protected by the regime for political reasons. Contracts can be completed successfully and profitably without sacrificing integrity or professional image.

Before entering into a contract in a country with a dictator form of government, one should obtain all possible guarantees. First-class consultants should be retained to get good risk analysis as well as adequate political and commercial risk insurance coverage.

A company policy should be formulated to protect the organization and its employees from the whims of the client. No consultant wants to take a role as "police officer" for an international lending agency, but the job may be thrust upon the person inadvertently. If the client's staff is involved in unprofessional activities or wants to use the consultant in a way not intended by the loan agreement, the PM must have a "fallback" position. An example of this might be that a consultant's employee normally assigned to the position of adviser to the client's chief engineer (a position created by the World Bank for obvious reasons) could be ordered by the client to take on a task not related to the project. By doing so, the chief engineer probably intended to show that the Bank-imposed adviser was really not needed. The PM should be alert to recognize when he is being used or bypassed, and have a planned course of action—a chat with the lending agency's local representative will remind the client of the consultant's proper role.

Often the PM will find a local mentor to be of great help. The local associate may fill this need, but normally it would be better to locate someone with no direct interest in the client or the project. In a Latin American country, social friendships with a British accountant and a local businessman proved valuable in providing understanding of the local politics. Their invaluable backgrounding served well in some delicate situations on a difficult assignment.

It is hard to imagine an architect-engineer or a construction manager knowingly accepting a contract that will expose the firm or its employees to terrorism. In these times, however, conditions change rapidly and exporters should be aware. Waiting for a flight to Tehran in the Athens airport on a beautiful summer day in 1973, my wife and I were on the fringes of a terrorist shooting spree which resulted in ten killed and over fifty wounded. Tourists, airline employees, passengers, businesspeople, and spectators were the victims. Being involved in international business had nothing to do with exposure to this risk. Today, a terrorist attack could break out in almost any major city.

A firm taking a new design contract in an apparently tranquil country plans occasional visits by professional teams and management during the preconstruction phase. When the project advances to the construction phase, the consultant may station a supervisory staff on the site for a long period. A very good relationship of trust and confidence—the consultant's prime objective—develops with the client. Prospects for more work look good. If suddenly world conditions change and the project country turns into a war zone, the client may want the project to continue and the consultant to remain on the job. The consultant's commitment to overseas operations may become strained as management begins to question the wisdom of trying to stay the course. The history of firms which have done business for many years in areas recently struck by turmoil, making consulting operations difficult, shows many of them adjust successfully when they are needed. One finds consultants enduring in such places as Tripoli, Libya; Lagos, Nigeria; Baghdad, Iraq; Panama; Santiago, Chile; Kuwait; and Buenos Aires, Argentina. British firms seem particularly good at maintaining outposts and coming up with contracts in countries which most design professionals have deleted from their marketing programs.

The longer a resourceful consulting firm stays in the international market, the less its management will tend to panic at reports of political unrest. Over time, the ability to analyze risk develops in the international staff, enabling it to make decisions rationally rather than being governed by the emotions of one individual member.

The international market for design services will offer opportunities seeded with risks—political unrest, wars, and terrorism. Even the most conservative management can find that what had seemingly been a "quiet" area has rapidly degraded into a war zone (like Beirut). An alert PM, aided by political risk and security consultants, will produce an operations plan to cope with changing conditions. By fully developing a relationship with the local associate, as well as with a local personal mentor, this man on the scene can form sound conclusions and keep top management correctly advised of the changing commercial and personal risk. Developing the strength of this capacity pays off when the time comes for the consultant to make the big decision: whether to stay or go.

# CHAPTER 20

# PHILOSOPHY AND GOALS

A rational method for planning and implementing international operations for a design-related organization was presented in preceding chapters. Rather than following a "cookbook" approach, I have discussed basic principles as well as the best methods for first testing the export market and then conducting foreign operations. Emphasis has been placed on homework, cross-cultural relations, and design quality control.

International operations require greater investments of time and personal attention than other areas of professional design practice. An awareness of what is happening and ability to get along with other cultures are crucial to success. And more difficult challenges must be overcome: Hostile environments must be neutralized; a strong interest in and a persistent effort to train foreign staff must be maintained.

Positive approaches to the great international market have been stressed throughout the text. Eventually, even the most dedicated internationalist may ask, "What am I doing here, anyway? Why didn't I take Mother's advice and become an English teacher?" Such questions of self-doubt surface at anguishing moments: when one is lying on the floor of the Athens airport during a terrorist attack; while a noisy mob in Lagos,

Nigeria, chants "Death to Kissinger"; or when a French contractor is railing about the unrivaled quality of his concrete, just rejected.

But the professional and cultural rewards are so compelling that these fleeting doubts are soon dispelled by the realities. If there is one outstanding trait that marks the international design professional, it is enthusiasm for change. Most veterans seem to radiate satisfaction and eagerness to move on to undertake the next project. Some international design firms, like Doxiadis Associates of Athens, Greece, periodically survey senior staff to determine which contracts offered them the most professional satisfaction. Using rating scales, each person assigned to a contract graded it periodically. Even the more pedestrian chores provided satisfaction in the international market because new environments and cultures were involved. (This may account for the appeal of Peace Corps assignments to young professionals.) In spite of an overbearing client, high altitudes, and what the foreign service would call a "hardship" post, it was not surprising to find that most of my fellow expatriates assigned to a highway program in Latin America would have offered to work only for expenses if they had no family obligations. Yes, the allure of an international project for expatriate professionals is enormous.

Romantic writers used to attribute insobriety, laziness, and incompetence to peripatetic construction and engineering personnel. There may have been some validity to that years ago. But my personal assessment of overseas staff in recent years is that the pace is as fast and the quality of performance as high as it is at home. Innovators, entrepreneurs, diplomats, and teachers find themselves to be in universal demand in the international market. Particularly in developing countries, the architects and engineers in the international design field have the added challenge of making their concepts work in new environments and cultures.

In the export market, even getting to the site may present a challenge. Labor usually requires housing, feeding, clothing, and training. One might begin with teaching workers not to dig with a machete but to use a long-handled shovel. Wearing shoes, hard hats, and protective clothing will be unacceptable to some cultures. Instead of subcontracting specialty items, contractors will be concerned with vocational training, provision of hand tools, and safety instructions.

The expatriate professional will find the challenges in the

planning and design functions to be comparable to those confronting the expatriate contractor. An exception might be that in some foreign markets the training and educational efforts of local and foreign professionals have produced a legacy of qualified engineers. One can sense the competency of personnel trained by the U.S. Bureau of Public Roads in Panama and Central America, by the U.S. Bureau of Reclamation in Mexico, by American oil companies in Venezuela and Peru, and by mining companies in Chile.

Generally, however, a major portion of the consultant's effort in foreign operations must be devoted to training. Although less time will be spent on basic design and field procedures and more on management decision making and contract administration, the educational role remains a substantial obligation. In fact, there is a tendency on the part of increasingly sophisticated clients and the international lending agencies to include a heavy training component in all large design and construction management contracts.

The ability of the consultant to transfer professional and management skills to a client's staff of course depends on the availability of trainable personnel. Increased attention is being paid to this problem and to claims by developing countries that foreign consulting firms leave little behind them in the way of transferred technical skills.

The ever-present challenges of overseas practice increase as the professional class grows in each developing country. In fact, the edge in making a successful proposal may now be found in a very carefully structured offer of realistic "hands-on" training for the client's staff. The day-to-day operation of a design office abroad will turn out to be a teaching experience. If the local associate's office is involved, the training aspect may be more subtle. But in the end the philosophy of passing on the torch and working oneself out of the job will be instilled in all of the consultant's expatriate staff.

The international consultant's role is one of building a bridge between cultures. In another sense it is building a bridge between the theoretical ideal and the best obtainable product. Dedicated professionals who elect to stay in the export market will ponder this aspect for the remainder of their professional careers. Elementary items like concrete finish on tunnel linings, bridge piers, and building facades will cause wrinkles and gray hair, if not ulcers, in the most resilient of PMs. For example, trying to enforce U.S. government standards for surface smoothness of a concrete tunnel lining in the mountains of Nicaragua on a project designed by an Italian consultant and built by a French contractor with local labor would almost produce schizophrenia in an otherwise normal person. The end result must be a compromise, if the project is ever to be completed.

There are many similar situations where the PM must bring to bear all the possible patience, skill, and training to build that "bridge to reality." The guiding principle is to avoid sacrificing engineering and construction standards while maintaining a position of control over the quality of the entire project and dealing effectively with the environment. New challenges will come at every turn. This promise alone attracts resourceful personalities.

The professional satisfaction of operating in the foreign market defies definition. If enthusiasm is the hallmark of the international consultant, job satisfaction must run a close second. A theory has been developed concerning the identification of individual consulting engineers, and I frequently apply tests of this theory, to while away the time on long international flights. Clothing and haircuts run to conservative taste. Practical yet elegant leather attaché cases with "frequent flyer" or first-class airline club tags also are good clues. But the dead giveaway comes on reaching cruising altitude, when the subject opens a battered attaché case, revealing programmable calculator, travel alarm with world time zones, microcassette dictating machine, and pocket airline guide. The antacid tablets, prescription drugs, and all the remedies for occupational ailments may also surface. But when one enters into conversation with those peripatetic professionals—either before or after they start checking proposals or completing expense accounts—the characteristics which they exude are enthusiasm and job satisfaction. In several instances a well-worn set of plans has eventually emerged to draw a small group of intense spectators gathering around to hear how the rapids were harnessed, or how the bow mooring device was completed in time for the first shipment of crude oil, or how the Apollo tracking station was put on the air on schedule. Yes, the international consultant is amply rewarded with an interesting professional life.

Material rewards in the export market are in keeping with responsibilities and the hardships, as they must be to attract necessary talent. In addition to salary and perquisites, which are influenced by labor market conditions and personal negotiation with management, there is another major factor. The management training offered by a PM assignment will often lead to entrepreneurial opportunities in the form of a partnership, corporate officer status, and stock ownership. Because foreign service does not appeal to some who feel more comfortable at home cultivating roses or being half of a two-career family, international management positions are frequently difficult to fill from the ranks. This is another reason why foreign assignments frequently lead to accelerated career advancement. In summary, enthusiasm, professional and material reward, and career advancement await the well-qualified professional in the export market.

What about future business prospects in the export market? Is export demand stable, growing, or declining? When a target country has been identified, how long will opportunities last— how does one cope with a cyclical market? If answers to these questions could be obtained by some exotic formula, not much discussion about foreign operations would be needed. But the export market reacts to so many diverse influences and pressures that forecasting demands is a franchise properly left to witch doctors, dowsers, and readers of tea leaves. Lacking scientific solutions, one must resort to the next best alternative— the "business school" method of examining case histories. The following three cases illustrate the most common experiences:

- **Easy Picking.** A U.S. AID contract in Nigeria is awarded to an American architectural and engineering firm. It being the firm's first project in the country, the organization has no knowledge of Nigeria's culture, economy, politics, or environment. The contract is designed in America with job-site visits by teams of home office engineers and architects, plus one or two annual visits by a vice president. No real contacts are made with local business or government, partly because the company is not registered commercially or professionally and it pays no Nigerian taxes. It makes no serious marketing efforts, so establishes no presence. No real local association results. Yet management believes that the company has valuable experience in Nigeria, and its brochures seem to say so. When the AID contract is completed, random marketing efforts are made by project-related personnel, because of the interest in Nigeria. But as it establishes neither a management commitment nor a local presence, the sporadic marketing attempts produce no results; the firm abandons this market.

Many other firms have similar experiences in foreign operations. Their first project in a new market was awarded without any experience or association in the project country, probably because of a client relationship developed with a lending agency on previous contracts and a solid record for quality and completion. But because there was no real commitment to marketing and no effort to establish an association with a local professional or a legal presence in the country, the market dried up at the end of the first contract or two. One can liken the experience to what happens when a person picks the fruit from the lowest branches only—a short-sighted plan at best.

■ *The Honeymoon That Doesn't Last.*  After a well-planned market approach and taking all the recommended steps for fact finding, associate selection, and establishing a representative office, the thus committed architectural and engineering firm is awarded several contracts in a new country. A strong presence is established, and the company has a good record of professional and financial success. But after five years or more, the bloom seems to fade from the market. Competition from international firms with lower costs reduces fee scales considerably. The rise of the local professional class leads to laws requiring that increasingly large amounts of the design effort be accomplished by local firms and that the consulting firm also increase design staff in the country. Eventually, the national infrastructure program winds down, and contract awards become scarce as demand for petroleum slackens, revenues drop, and planning and design programs suffer. When political unrest or war develops, it has drastic effect on opportunities for international design firms. (Libya, Saudi Arabia, Lebanon, and Latin American countries have gone through this cycle.) The well-established architect-engineer's future then looks bleak. What to do to survive? Should the office be closed as contracts are completed? Should the architect-engineer enter the price wars just to get a contract to pay part of the overhead, and attempt to ride out the depressed market?

Knowing what to do when the honeymoon is over is one of the consultant's biggest challenges. Worst-case scenarios must be developed. It is a truism that good markets are perishable. International operations are affected by many forces not present (or at least not expected) at home. No foreign operation should be undertaken without contingency plans for coping with sudden changes in the market.

- *Winners and Losers.* Not all contracts are financial winners. It is a fact of life that there will be international projects
which even the best organization, the finest PM, and the strong-
est financial backing cannot salvage. The telltale clues will be
evident early, when the client becomes impossible to please,
competent staff resigns, costs rise, and percentage of completion stagnates. The contract may have been negotiated at too
low a price or the scope of work may be controversial or the
client difficult to deal with. In any case, the net result is loss of
profit and satisfaction. All these unfavorable factors can occur
despite a competent staff and high-quality technical performance.

The PM must determine the true reason for the loss situation. It is a lonesome duty, because the staff will become protective and the client will not accept any blame. Herculean
efforts will be required just to cut losses. Frequently, key personnel must be shifted to eliminate personality conflicts. All
reasonable effort should be made to retain the client's goodwill,
but the chances of more work may be quite dim. A losing contract usually means the end of a client relationship, and all the
marketing skills available will not change this conclusion.
When the handwriting on the wall is legible, the worst-case scenario—finishing the job, cutting overheads, and getting on to
fairer climates—should be implemented.

Benefiting from rising design and construction markets
might be likened to speculating in the stock market. Investors
try to get into a market at the beginning of a rise and to sell on
or before a downturn—it sounds very simple. If the stock market is unpredictable, the design and construction market in
developing countries is certainly more so. In spite of very
sophisticated systems, some of the best-known consultants
have shaky track records on predictions. When a given market
has run its course because of political and economic reasons or
just because demands have been satisfied, the international
consultant must be prepared to make the big decisions. Alternate markets will have been thoroughly and discreetly
researched. Retrenchment of overhead costs should begin and
senior staff should be prepared for transfer.

If management is committed to return to the country or
market region when conditions improve, there may be great
merit in leaving behind a representative office that will act as a
listening post and "fly the flag." One frequently meets solitary

partners and officers of large consulting firms in depressed market areas who are waiting for better times. British and European firms seem to be more patient than others in this regard, patrolling the Middle East, Africa, and Latin America, hoping to take prompt advantage of economic and political changes. Historically, representatives of other countries, such as the United States, arrive on the scene after the "gold rush" starts.

A continual effort, rationally planned, should be directed to the task of detecting market shift. The job is one which can be done best by a sensitive senior officer, and does not lend itself to a committee effort. Knowing when to look for new markets, when to stay the course, and when to abandon a market will be the stuff that separates the successful firms from the rest of the competition. The goal is to keep the low spots out of the firm's business cycle and to maintain management commitment to the international market.

When the decision is made to move out of a market there should be no need for panic or grief. The plan for closing down will have been worked out in detail with the help of legal and accounting consultants. Local employees who are not offered employment in another foreign operation or at the home office should be terminated in strict conformance with local laws and company policy, whichever is better for the individual. A serious effort could be made to place all employees who are being released with other firms. All accounts should be paid. A legal representative must be appointed to be the firm's agent in any claim that may arise after closing. In summary, the exodus should be made in the most professional style possible, so the firm's return will be welcomed should economic conditions improve.

The success of any effort is enhanced by setting goals. One hears sports professionals exhorting players to establish goals—never to hit a golf ball or throw a baseball without picking a target or to swim a lap without a time to beat. Goals, to be worthwhile, should cause an extension of effort while being attainable. International operations should be directed toward realistic goals. For instance, a goal for a design firm might be to provide 30 percent of the annual sales from foreign markets. And since, as discussed, risks are greater in the international markets than at home, the profit goal might be to derive 40 percent of the firm's annual total profit from foreign sales. Realistic long-term goals can be established along these lines by the management after the first market studies are completed.

I recall a large architectural and engineering firm whose management was obsessed with size. Its oft-stated long-range goal was to be the largest design firm in the country. Another goal was to enter only into contracts which the board of directors considered to be "fun." Neither of these two ambitions appear realistic. Bigness in itself has nothing to do with professional satisfaction, quality, and a fair return on investment. It also developed that the board's definition of "fun" frequently conflicted with the interpretation placed on the same word by senior staff and clients. To the staff, attainable profit goals, establishment of a sound professional reputation, and professional satisfaction were much more important.

Little has been said in this book about salaries, profit sharing, and fringe benefits for employees. If it is accepted that a successful firm must attract good professional talent and provide them with attractive working conditions, then the compensation and benefits program must be structured accordingly. Within the industry, supply and demand regulate the ebbs and flows of the different forms of compensation.

Short-range goals for the day-to-day management of an international operation are most easily achieved by following these cardinal rules:

- Begin with homework; then proceed with fact finding.
- Obtain management commitment.
- Select high-quality associates.
- Set attainable goals.
- Develop cross-cultural understanding.
- Assign a competent professional as your representative on the scene.
- Prepare for market change.
- Avoid local politics.
- Establish and maintain personal ethics.
- Work with enthusiasm.

The project managers, foreign representatives, and senior staff of international consultant firms are frequently examples of the Renaissance men and women of our times.

# SOURCE MATERIALS

**BIBLIOGRAPHY**

Blanchard, Kenneth H., and Spencer Johnson: *The One Minute Manager*, Berkley, New York, 1983.

Caudill, William Wayne: *Architecture by Team*, Van Nostrand Reinhold, New York, 1971.

*Guidelines for the Use of Consultants by World Bank Borrowers and by the World Bank as an Executing Agency*, World Bank, Washington, D.C., 1981.

Levine, Irving R.: *Main Street, Italy*, Doubleday, Garden City, N.Y., 1963.

McCreary, Edward A.: *The Americanization of Europe*, Doubleday, Garden City, N.Y., 1964.

Peters, Thomas J., and Robert H. Waterman, Jr.: *In Search of Excellence*, Harper & Row, New York, 1982.

Stokes, McNeill: *International Construction Contracts*, 2d ed., Engineering News-Record, New York.

**OTHER INFORMATION RESOURCES**

African Development Bank, Boite Postale 1387, Abidjan, Ivory Coast.

American Institute of Architects (AIA), 1735 New York Avenue, NW, Washington, DC 20005.

American Management Association, 135 West 50th Street, New York, NY 10020.

Arabian American Oil Company (ARAMCO), P.O. Box 5000, Dhahran, Saudi Arabia.

Area handbooks—prepared for the U.S. Army by the Foreign Area Studies Institute of American University, Washington, D.C. for most of the countries in the world. Available from the Superintendent of Documents, U.S. Government Printing Office, Washington, DC 20402.

Asian Development Bank, P.O. Box 789, Manila, Philippines.

Atlantic Richfield Company (ARCO), 515 South Flower Street, Los Angeles, CA 90071.

Barclays Bank of New York, 200 Park Avenue, New York, NY 10017.

Blount, Inc., 4520 Executive Park Drive, Montgomery, AL 36116.

*Business America*—bi-weekly publication of the U.S. Department of Commerce, Washington, DC 20230.

The Business Council for International Understanding Institute, American University, 3301 New Mexico Avenue, NW, Washington, DC 20016.

Chamber of Commerce of the United States, International Division, 1615 H Street, NW, Washington, DC 20062. Contact for addresses of American chambers of commerce in specific countries.

Chase Manhattan Bank, One Chase Plaza, New York, NY 10081.

Citibank, NA, 399 Park Avenue, New York, NY 10043.

*Commerce Business Daily*—published by the U.S. Department of Commerce. Order from the Superintendent of Documents, U.S. Government Printing Office, Washington, DC 20402.

*Daily Telegraph*, Daily Telegraph Limited, 135 Fleet Street, London EC4, England. Features international tender announcements, contracting and engineering news, and classified advertisements.

*Development Forum Business Edition*, DFBE Liaison Unit, World Bank, 1818 H Street, NW, Washington, DC 20433.

Doxiadis Associates International Group, S.A., P.O. Box 471, Athens, Greece.

Dun and Bradstreet (D & B), 99 Church Street, New York, NY 10007.

The Economist, 10 Rockefeller Plaza, New York, NY 10020.

*Embassy Post Report*—a report of living conditions at each U.S. State Department foreign post.

*Engineering News-Record*, McGraw-Hill Publications Company, 1221 Avenue of the Americas, New York, NY 10020.

Ernst and Whinney, 153 East 53rd Street, New York, NY 10032.

Esso Research and Engineering Company, P.O. Box 101, Florham Park, NJ 07932.

Export-Import Bank of the United States (Ex-Im Bank), 811 Vermont Avenue, NW, Washington, DC 20503.

Exxon Corporation, 1251 Avenue of the Americas, New York, NY 10020.

Foreign Corrupt Practices Act—information available from the U.S. Department of Justice, Tenth Street and Constitution Avenue, NW, Washington, DC 20530.

Foreign Economic Trends and Their Implications for the United States (FET). Available from the Superintendent of Documents, U.S. Government Printing Office, Washington, DC 20402.

The Financial Times, Bracken House, Cannon Street, London EC4P 4BY, England.

Fluor Corporation, 3333 Michelson Drive, Irvine, CA 92730.

French, Martin, Rozen Rust, Oude Trambaan 5, 2265 CA, Leidshendam, The Netherlands.

General Accounting Office (GAO), 441 G Street, NW, Washington, DC 20548.

Harper and Shuman, Inc., 68 Moulton Street, Cambridge, MA 02138.

Inter-American Development Bank, 808 Seventeenth Street, NW, Washington, DC 20577.

Internal Revenue Service (IRS), 1111 Constitution Avenue, NW, Washington, DC 20244.

International Colombian Resources Corporation (INTERCOR), Bogotá, Colombia.

International Construction Week—published by Engineering News-Record, McGraw-Hill Publications Company, 1221 Avenue of the Americas, New York, NY 10020.

International Engineering Committee, American Consulting Engineers Council, 1015 15th Street, NW, Washington, DC 20005, Attn: Director of International Affairs.

International Federation of Consulting Engineers (FIDIC), P.O. Box 86, CH-1000, Lausanne, 12-Chailly, Switzerland.

KLM—Royal Dutch Airlines, 437 Madison Avenue, New York, NY 10036.

Lloyds of London, Lloyds Building, Lime Street, London EC3, England.

Marine Midland Bank, 140 Broadway, New York, NY 10015.

Middle East Economic Digest (MEED), c/o Powers International, 551 Fifth Avenue, New York, NY 10176.

Mobil Oil Corporation, 150 East 42nd Street, New York, NY 10017.

*Monthly Operational Summary, Development Forum—Business Edition*, DFBE Liaison Unit, World Bank, 1818 H Street, NW, Washington, DC 20433.

Morgan Guaranty Trust Company, 23 Wall Street, New York, NY 10015.

National Geographic Society, 1145 Seventeenth Street, NW, Washington, DC 20036.

National Society of Professional Engineers (NSPE), 1420 King Street, Alexandria, VA 22314.

New York Times Company, 229 West 43rd Street, New York, NY 10036.

Occidental Petroleum Corporation, 10889 Wilshire Boulevard, Los Angeles, CA 90024.

*Overseas Business Reports* (OBR)—Available from the Superintendent of Documents, U.S. Government Printing Office, Washington, DC 20402.

Overseas Private Investment Corporation (OPIC) (an agency of the United States Government), 1129 20th Street, NW, Washington, DC 20527.

Price Waterhouse and Company, 1257 Avenue of the Americas, New York, NY 10020.

Raider, Ellen, Ellen Raider International, Incorporated, 752 Carroll Street, Brooklyn, NY 11215—produces *International Negotiations—A Training Program for Corporate Executives and Diplomats with Situations Management, Inc.*

Situations Management, Inc., 121 Sandwich Street, Plymouth, MA 02360 (see Raider, Ellen).

*State Department Background Notes*—available for specific foreign countries from the Superintendent of Documents, U.S. Government Printing Office, Washington, DC 20402.

Tennessee Valley Authority (TVA), 400 Commerce Avenue, Knoxville, TN 37902.

United Nations Educational, Scientific and Cultural Organization (UNESCO), First Avenue and 42nd Street, New York, NY 10017.

U.S. Agency for International Development (USAID), Department of State, Washington, DC 20523.

U.S. Army Corps of Engineers, Office, Chief of Engineers, Washington, DC 20314.

U.S. Department of Commerce, International Trade Administration, 14th Street and Constitution Avenue, NW, Washington, DC 20230.

U.S. Naval Facilities Engineering Command, Department of the Navy, 200 Stovall Street, Alexandria, VA 22332.

U.S. Peace Corps, 806 Connecticut Avenue, NW, Washington, DC 20526.

*Wall Street Journal,* Dow Jones Publishing Company, 22 Cortlandt Street, New York, NY 10007.

World Bank (The International Bank for Reconstruction and Development and the International Development Association), 1818 H Street, NW, Washington, DC 20433.

*Worldwide Projects*—published by Intercontinental Publications, P.O. Box 5017, Westport, CT 06880.

## ABOUT THE AUTHOR

Chester L. Lucas has worked as a professional engineer for over forty-five years. Beginning foreign service in 1940 as a U.S. Army field engineer at the Panama Canal, he has headed offices in such countries as Panama, Ecuador, Italy, and Greece. Lucas's responsibilities have incorporated all aspects of an architect-engineer's organization—from design and operations to marketing and financial management—on national highway programs, town planning, public works, military installations, and housing. With a BSCE degree from Duke University, his most recent position was as International Vice President of Sverdrup Corporation in St. Louis. Lucas, now semiretired, is a consultant to architects, engineers, and contractors with international operations.

# INDEX